# GATES

## Thanksgiving Papers

David Niedenfuer

**Gates:  Thanksgiving Papers**
by *David Niedenfuer*

Signalman Publishing
www.signalmanpublishing.com
email: info@signalmanpublishing.com
Kissimmee, Florida

ISBN: 978-1-940145-00-6

Library of Congress Control Number: 2013938938

Unless otherwise indicated, Bible quotations are taken from The King
James Version (KJV) of the Holy Bible.

Scripture quotations noted NIV are from the HOLY BIBLE: NEW IN-
TERNATIONL VERSION®. Copyright © 1973, 1978, 1984 by Interna-
tional Bible Society.  Used by permission of Zondervan Publishing House.
All rights reserved.

Scripture quotations noted NKJV are from THE NEW KING JAMES
VERSION.  Copyright © 1979,1980,1982,1990, 1994 by Thomas Nelson,
Inc.

Scripture quotations noted AMP are taken from the Amplified® Bible,
Copyright © 1954, 1958, 1962, 1964, 1965, 1987 by The Lockman Foundation. Used by permission. (www.Lockman.org).

Signalman
Publishing

*I dedicate this book to my Lord and Savior, Jesus Christ, who is my Life and my Friend. I also dedicate this book to my wife, Nina. I am truly blessed with a wonderful God-given wife and help-mate. Your encouragement and help have really aided me in writing this book.*

# Table of Contents

Introduction. . . . . . . . . . . . . . . . . . . . . . . . . . . . . . . .6

One: Children of Promise. . . . . . . . . . . . . . . . . . . . . 9

Two: The Gates. . . . . . . . . . . . . . . . . . . . . . . . . . . . 51

Three: Imaginations. . . . . . . . . . . . . . . . . . . . . . . . .83

Four: Repentance-No Gamble. . . . . . . . . . . . . . . .100

Conclusion. . . . . . . . . . . . . . . . . . . . . . . . . . . . . . .104

Faith Comes by Hearing. . . . . . . . . . . . . . . . . . . . 106

Salvation Prayer. . . . . . . . . . . . . . . . . . . . . . . . . .108

Bibliography. . . . . . . . . . . . . . . . . . . . . . . . . . . . . 109

# Introduction

"Open for me the gates of righteousness; I will enter and give thanks to the LORD."
—Psalm 118:19 NIV

What is a gate but a portal that allows entrance or exit from one place to another?

Jesus said, "Very truly I tell you, whoever hears my word and believes him who sent Me has eternal life and will not be judged, but has crossed over from death to life." (John 5:24 NIV)

Jesus came to bring us life and life more abundantly. Jesus is all about life. He is Life. He came to bring us life because *that's what we needed*. We needed life because, as the Word of God tells us, mankind's problem is that we are "spiritually dead." To be "spiritually dead" means to be spiritually separated from God.

This is a stark reality that no amount of good works or good behavior will remedy, for as God said through the Apostle Paul, "…for if there had been a law given which could have **given life,** verily righteousness should have been by the law." (Gal. 3:21b) (and) "But now the righteousness of God without the law is manifested, being witnessed by the law and the prophets; Even the righteousness of God which is by faith of Jesus Christ unto all and upon all them that believe:"… (Rom. 3:21-22a) (emphasis mine).

Fortunately, it's not our behavior Father God is looking at, but His Son's, who was sent to die for us as a sacrificial offering. He laid down His life so we can receive life, the life He now freely offers. This book is about the *life* God offers and the *freedom* we enter into once we receive it, how we must *defend this freedom by guarding our thought lives*, and the joy and thankfulness we experience when we do.

My hope in writing this book is to convey the freedom we've entered into as Christians and how we as individual believers must choose which thoughts we allow to gain access to our hearts and which ones [thoughts] we will reject. In order to make the correct choice, we must know the truth so we can **reject the lies** that try to come against it.

# ONE

## Children of Promise

The Apostle Paul uses the epistle of Galatians to make perhaps his most passionate statements against preaching a "wrong gospel" or a different gospel (see Gal. 1:6-7). He then proceeds further in the epistle and asks these questions of the Galatians: "This only would I learn of you, Received ye the Spirit by the works of the law, or by the hearing of faith? Are ye so foolish? Having begun in the Spirit, are ye now made perfect by the flesh?" (Gal. 3:2-3)

The NIV phrases it this way: "I would like to learn just one thing from you: Did you receive the Spirit by observing the law, or by believing what you heard? Are you so foolish? After beginning with the Spirit, are you now trying to attain your goal by human effort?" (Gal. 3:2-3)

In the previous Scripture verses, Paul is, of course, referencing the question as to how they became born again, because that's when they received the Holy Spirit. Before you were born again, you were "spiritually dead" and receiving the Spirit of God is what brought you eternal life. The answer that the Apostle Paul wanted to hear from the Galatians was that before they were born again, they were spiritually dead and no amount of *good works* or *human effort* would change that. It was only by hearing the message of the gospel, and believing it, that they received the Spirit and became born again. This answer would have satisfied Paul, but he knew that some people were trying to subvert the true gospel, telling and teaching the Galatians that they had to add works to what Christ had done, in order to be saved. This infuriated Paul, and it should us, as well.

### Which One is Your Mother?

Further in this epistle, Paul goes on to say,

> Tell me, you who want to be under the law, are you not aware of what the law says? For it is written that Abraham had two sons, one by the slave woman, and the other by the free woman. His son by the slave woman was born in the ordinary way; but his son by the free woman was born as the result of *a promise*. These things may be taken figuratively, for the women represent two covenants. One covenant is from Mount Sinai and bears children who are to be slaves: This is Hagar. Now Hagar stands for Mount Sinai in Arabia and corresponds to the present city of Jerusalem, because she is in slavery with her children. But the

Jerusalem that is above is free, **and she is
our mother**. (Gal. 4:21-26 NIV, emphasis
mine)

These scriptures are profound because the Apostle
Paul is telling us that Abraham had two sons; the first
being Ishmael, who was born by Abraham and Sarah's
handmaid, Hagar. Hagar represents the Covenant of
law; the Covenant which is from Mount Sinai. Ishmael had been born in the natural way.

Isaac, Abraham's second son, was a **child of promise** and born by the power of the Spirit. (Remember,
Abraham and Sarah were well beyond their child-bear-
ing years. It was a true miracle for them to produce a
child.) Sarah represents grace and the New Covenant
put into effect by Jesus. Now this is really awesome
because God is telling us that we who are "born again"
are like Isaac; we too are children of the promise (see
Gal. 4:28).

So what does he say?

Now you, brothers, like Isaac, are children
of promise. At that time, the son born in
the ordinary way persecuted the son born
by the power of the Spirit. It is the same
now. But what does the scripture say? "Get
rid of the slave woman and her son, for the
slave woman's son will never share in the
inheritance with the free woman's son."
Therefore, brothers, we are not children of
the slave woman, but of the free woman.
(Gal. 4:28-31 NIV1984)

Here, God is using Paul, in effect, to tell us that we [we who are born again] have the same Father, who, of course, is Father God, our heavenly Father, but not all of us [we who are born again] are choosing the same *mother.* Some Christians are choosing to be brought up by Hagar, who represents the law, and some Christians are choosing to be brought up by Sarah, who represents **grace**.

But once again, what does the Scripture say?

> Get rid of the slave woman and her son, for the slave woman's son will never share in the inheritance with the free woman's son. Therefore, brothers and sisters, we are not children of the slave woman, but of the free woman. (Gal. 4:30b-31 NIV)

In other words, Sarah, who represents grace, is well able to raise us up [we who are born-again Christians] and we are to cast out Hagar and her son, who represent the law and natural birth.

This is the reason for the following verse in Galatians which says: "Stand fast therefore *in the liberty* wherewith Christ hath made us free, and be not entangled again with the yolk of bondage." (Gal. 5:1, italics mine)

It's up to us as individual born-again Christians to personally **choose** not to be entangled again with the yolk of bondage… which is *the law.*

### *Our Need for Righteousness*

I believe most Christians who are truly born again understand that before they were saved, they were unable, on their own merit or human effort, to make themselves worthy of salvation. They understood why they needed a Savior and they accepted His sacrificial atonement for their sin. As it's often said, "Come as you are, with all your faults." This is what those of us who are born again did. We heard the message of the gospel, which speaks of a righteousness from God, apart from law, which is given through faith in Jesus Christ to all who believe (see Rom. 3:21-22).

We did this through belief and confession, for it is stated in Paul's letter to the Romans:

> That if thou shalt confess with thy mouth the Lord Jesus, and shalt believe in thine heart that God hath raised Him from the dead, thou shalt be saved. For with the heart **man believeth unto righteousness;** and with the mouth confession is made unto salvation. For the Scripture saith, WHOSOEVER BELIEVETH ON HIM SHALL NOT BE ASHAMED.

> For there is no difference between the Jew and the Greek: for the same Lord over all is rich unto all that call upon Him. FOR WHOSOEVER SHALL CALL UPON THE NAME OF THE LORD SHALL BE SAVED. (Rom. 10:9-13, emphasis mine)

So when we received salvation, we also received the gift of righteousness (see Rom. 5:17). Just what does "righteousness" mean and why did we need to receive it as a gift? For as Romans 5:16 &17 tell us, "justification comes **through a 'gift' of righteousness**." [author's paraphrase] One definition of "justice" found in the New Webster's Concise Dictionary of the English Language, (2003 ed.) is: "the quality of being just, fair, or impartial; even-handedness." The word "righteous" comes from a root word: "just" or "authority to uphold what is right." "Righteous" means "acting in accord with divine or moral law: free from guilt or sin." (2012 Merriam Webster, Inc.)

Righteousness [noun form], in reference to man, refers to that which is required from man by God. The law demands righteousness *from* sinful man; whereas grace imparts righteousness *to* sinful man. Under law, everything depended upon man and his obedience, but under grace everything depends upon Jesus and what he did on the cross. We needed it [righteousness] as a free gift because everything mentioned in the definitions referenced above, we were found to be lacking in God's eyes, or you could say… we came up short (see Rom. 3:23). We had no hope of keeping the **righteous requirements** of the law (see Rom. 8:4) on our own merit or human effort.

Jesus said in His Sermon on the Mount, "Be perfect, therefore, as your heavenly Father is perfect." (Mat. 5:48 NIV) It's found elsewhere in Scripture: "For whosoever shall keep the whole law, and yet offend in one point, he is guilty of all." (James 2:10)

How did we, as mankind, find ourselves in this predicament, and how did the gift of righteousness aid us?

Well, the Apostle Paul explains in the book of Romans:

> But not as the offense, so also is the free gift. For if through the offense of one many be dead, much more the grace of God, and the gift by grace, *which* is by one man, Jesus Christ, hath abounded unto many. And not as *it was* by one that sinned, *so is* the gift: for the judgment was by one to condemnation, **but the free gift is of many offences unto justification**. For if by one man's offense death reigned by one; much more they which receive abundance of grace and of the gift of righteousness shall reign in life by one, Jesus Christ. Therefore as by the offense of one - *judgment came* upon all men to condemnation; even so by the righteousness of one *the free gift came* upon all men **unto justification of life**. For as by one man's disobedience many were made sinners, so by the obedience of one shall many be made righteous. (Rom. 5:15-19, emphasis mine)

### *Our Need Was Life*

The Apostle Paul explained in the Scripture above that

because of one, "Adam," many are dead. By dead, he means spiritually un-alive or unregenerate. This was caused by the original sin in the Garden, (see Gen. 3:6-7) and along with sin came judgment, which brought condemnation, and along with condemnation came *death*. Now Adam and Eve lived for many years, physically, after the judgment was pronounced in the Garden, but that day [the day they sinned] they died spiritually, and since then, death has been passed on down through the blood line to all mankind who have been born in the natural way. It's inherited.

Now, we know from the Word of God that Adam and Eve were created in the image of God (see Gen. 1:27). They were spiritually alive and were not separated from God. But, with the fall in the Garden they became spiritually dead, resulting in separation from God; they were separated from the very life of God. The Bible says in Genesis 5:3: "When Adam had lived 130 years, he had a son in his own likeness, in *his own image*; and he named him Seth." (NIV, italics mine) This son of Adam, [Seth] who was born after the fall, who was born in Adam's image, was born "spiritually dead," because that's all that Adam could pass on. It was inherited from Adam and passed on down through mankind's tainted bloodline, which became that way because of the fall.

So, if Adam and Eve, our biological parents, fell into sin and the whole world inherited their sin problem, along with spiritual death, then we would need an antidote for it. But that's just the problem; we were dead in the water, with no way to correct this tainted blood on our own. All of our *good works* only dressed up a dead man. Try as we might; it's like putting makeup on a corpse. It's prettier, but it's still dead. If our inherited, tainted blood caused us to fall out of relationship with God, then where did this leave mankind? We had a great need with no way [in our own strength] to remedy it.

## *Our Need for a Sinless Redeemer*

This great need points to the need for the virgin birth of Jesus (see Isa. 9:6, Luke 1:35). Because of the virgin birth, Jesus; who is fully man and fully God, was born without sin. He led a sinless life. Now, once again, we had a Man on earth who was without sin. Mary's body acted solely as an incubator because Jesus was conceived of the Holy Spirit. Mary's tainted blood, which she inherited through the fall of Adam and Eve, was not passed on to Jesus. So, when Christ shed His innocent blood on the cross, for the sin of the world, it was accepted by Father God as the atoning blood for the sin of the world, thus removing mankind's sin problem and also removing mankind's death problem, which was a result of sin.

So, yes, Jesus did die to take away our sin, but He also rose to newness of life to be able to give "spiritual life" to those who were "spiritually dead," to those who put faith in Him, in His shed blood (see Rom. 3:25). Remember, Adam was created spiritually alive and became spiritually dead. Jesus was born spiritually alive and remained spiritually alive and led a sinless life. So when He gave up His life on the cross, it was His sinless life He laid down.

Jesus said, "I lay my life down, so that I might take it up again." And that's just what Jesus did. He took it up again (see John 10:17). The epistle to the Ephesians tells us we were raised with Him through the working of the power of God (see Eph. 2:6). So now, because of, or by the righteousness of One, Jesus Christ, the free gift came upon all men **unto justification of life** (see Rom. 5:18). For what is it that a dead man needs... but LIFE?

## *Justified and Righteous*

With the free gift of righteousness [right-standing with God], also came our inheritance from God: eternal life (see Rom. 6:23b). For as Jesus said, "Very truly I tell you, whoever hears my word and believes him who sent me has eternal life and will not be judged, but has crossed over **from death to life.**" (John 5:24 NIV, emphasis mine)

"Righteousness" signifies uprightness and right-standing with God. "Justified" refers to something that is crooked being made straight. In fact, we get the word "wicked" from the word "wicker"; meaning twisted. Once again, as stated in Romans, "Therefore as by the offense of one *judgment came* upon all men to condemnation; even so by the righteousness of One, *the free gift came* upon all men unto justification of life." (Rom. 5:18)

And when the Lord gives us His resurrected life, it can truly be eternal life because the only thing that could ever cause you to die [which is sin] has been completely dealt with at the cross.

Now the Apostle Paul tells us to offer ourselves to God as those who have been brought *from death to life*; and offer every part of ourselves to Him as instruments of righteousness (see Rom. 6:13). We are told through the Apostle Paul, in his epistle to the Romans that:

> It was not through the law that Abraham and his offspring received the promise that he would be heir of the world, but **through the righteousness that comes by faith**. For if those who depend on the law are heirs, faith means nothing and the promise is worthless, because the law brings wrath. And where there is no law there is no transgression. (Rom. 4:13-15 NIV, emphasis mine)

The Apostle Paul further states in his letter to the Galatians,

> But that no man is justified by the law in the sight of God, it is evident: for, The just shall live by faith. And the law is not of faith: but, The man that doeth them shall live in them. Christ hath redeemed us from the curse of the law, being made a curse for us: for it is written, Cursed is every one

that hangeth on a tree: That the blessing of Abraham might come on the Gentiles through Jesus Christ; that we might receive the promise of the Spirit through faith. (Gal. 3:11-14)

### *Instead of Fear... Sonship*

Paul goes on to say in his letter to the Romans: "Since we have now been justified by His blood, how much more shall we be saved from God's wrath through Him!" (Rom. 5:9 NIV)

Once again, further on, Paul states in his letter to the Romans: "The Spirit you received does not make you slaves, so that you live in fear again; rather, the Spirit you received brought about your adoption to sonship." "Now if we are children, we are heirs – heirs of God and co-heirs with Christ..." (Rom. 8:15a, 17a NIV). Now this is really cool. The Apostle Paul is saying in his letter to the Romans that the Spirit you received when you became born again does not make you slaves, so that you live in fear, but rather, the Spirit you received brought about your adoption to *sonship*. As Christians, we are sons and daughters of God.

If you have fear, this fear takes place in your mind. This fear is spoken of elsewhere in the epistle to the Hebrews. Scholars are uncertain as to who actually wrote the book of Hebrews. I believe it was Paul, but whomever it was, the Holy Spirit was speaking through him, saying:

Since the children have flesh and blood,

He too shared in their humanity, so that by His death He might break the power of him who holds the power of death – that is, the devil – and free those who all their lives were held in slavery by their fear of death. For surely it is not angels he helps, but Abraham's descendants. (Heb. 2:14-16 NIV)

Elsewhere, this fear is mentioned by the Apostle John in his first epistle, in which he uses this passage to talk about God's love, and this fear (see 1 John 4:7-21 for complete passage). John states here, "There is no fear in love. But perfect love drives out fear, because fear has to do with punishment. The one who fears is not made perfect in love." (1 John 4:18 NIV)

### *Unconditional Love*

This *perfect love* that drives out fear is mentioned in the book of Romans, where the Apostle Paul states, "But God demonstrates His own love for us in this: While we were still sinners, Christ died for us." (Rom. 5:8 NIV)

Why is it perfect love? Because it is **unconditional love**. So now, one might ask, "How did Jesus by His death break the power of him (satan) who held the power of death, and free those who all their lives were held in slavery by their fear of death, fear of spiritual death?" The answer is found in the book of Colossians, where once again, the Holy Spirit speaks through the

Apostle Paul saying,

> When you were dead in your sins and in
> the uncircumcision of your sinful nature,
> God made you *alive with Christ*. He for-
> gave us all our sins, having cancelled the
> written code, with its regulations that was
> against us and that stood opposed to us; He
> took it away, nailing it to the cross. And
> having disarmed the powers and authori-
> ties, He made a public spectacle of them,
> triumphing over them by the cross. (Col.
> 2:13-15 NIV, italics mine)

Now this is telling us that the written code, with
its regulations that were against us and that stood op-
posed to us, has been taken away. He took it away,
nailing it to the cross. This is referring to the "ten commandments" that were written with the finger of God.
And this is true. This did happen at the cross, but if
you or I had been there, nearly two thousand years
ago, the only thing we would have seen is Jesus [Love]
nailed to the cross.

But Jesus, who came to this earth, fully man and
fully God, was born "spiritually alive" and led a sinless life, and shed His holy blood that was the payment for the sin of the world. He was the first Man,
"fully man and fully God" to have never sinned, so
by His death He fulfilled the law (see Mat. 5:17). As
Scripture states, "For Christ is the end of the law for
righteousness to every one that believeth." (Rom 10:4)

## *The Life is in the Blood*

When Jesus said in the Sermon on the Mount, "Be ye therefore perfect, even as your Father which is in heaven is perfect," He was speaking to people who were under the Old Covenant of law. The law is unyielding and requires it be kept perfectly, and if not... a sacrifice must be made under the Levitical priesthood. As we find in Hebrews, "and without the shedding of blood, there is no forgiveness." (Heb. 9:22b NIV) This is also found in the book of Leviticus: "For the life of a creature is in the blood, and I have given it to you to make atonement for yourselves on the altar; it is the blood that makes atonement for one's life." (Lev. 17:11 NIV)

Under the Old Covenant, a proper sacrifice had to be made... or judgment came. The epistle written by James tells us, "For whosoever shall keep the whole law, and yet offend in one *point*, he is guilty of all." (James. 2:10)

But Jesus **did** keep the whole law; He fulfilled it. His sinless blood was shed. The animal sacrifices done in faith under the Old Covenant were a covering for sin, but they foreshadowed or looked forward, to the day when Christ would shed His blood on the cross; Jesus being the completely sufficient sacrifice for sin. So now, those who by faith appropriate the proper covering; Christ's shed blood, are acceptable before God, found completely *justified and righteous* (see Rom. 5:16-17).

Christ's blood is not only a covering, but it

completely washes us clean; whereas the animal sacrifices done in faith had to be repeated again and again, and offered only a temporal covering for sin. By looking to Jesus, by appropriating His work done on the cross, by receiving Him into our hearts, His very Spirit enters into us (see Acts 15:8). Through faith in what Jesus has done, we have access before God and true eternal Life living within us. Now once again, when Christ fulfilled the law and was nailed to the cross, He was crucified for our sin and resurrected *for our life.*

Now He is in heaven, seated at the right hand of God and will never die again. He's been raised to newness of life. Scripture tells us that we too, as believers, are seated with Christ in the heavenlies (see Eph. 2:6). It [Scripture] also tells us that we are one Spirit with Him (see 1 Cor. 6:17). This means that when we receive eternal life… it is truly eternal!

### *No More Fear*

Now this fear we discussed earlier, spoken of in the book of Hebrews, saying:

> Since the children have flesh and blood, He too shared in their humanity so that by His death He might break the power of him who holds the power of death – that is, the devil – and free those who all their lives were held in slavery by the fear of death. For surely it is not angels He helps,

but *Abraham's descendants.* (Heb. 2:14-16
NIV, italics mine)

This refers to us as believers. The fear that held us
in slavery and imprisoned us in hopelessness is now
broken. The power of him (satan) that bound us is
broken. Jesus did it by fulfilling the law through His
death and resurrection (see Rom. 10:4). Scripture tells
us that *we have died* to what once bound us, and we
have been released from the law, we died to the law, so
that we serve in the new way of the Spirit, and not in
the old way of the written code (see Rom. 7:6). The
Word tells us, "…you also died to the law through the
body of Christ," (Rom. 7:4a NIV).

It's stated earlier in the book of Romans, "It was not
through the law that Abraham and his offspring received the promise that he would be heir of the world,
but through the righteousness that comes by faith. For
if those who depend on the law are heirs, faith means
nothing and the promise is worthless, because the law
brings wrath. And where there is no law, there is no
transgression." (Rom. 4:13-15 NIV) Also found in
Hebrews, it's stated, "For there is verily a disannulling
of the commandment going before for the weakness
and unprofitableness thereof. For the law made nothing perfect, but the bringing in of a better hope *did;* by
the which we draw nigh unto God." (Heb. 7:18-19 )

When the Apostle John said in his epistle, "There is
no fear in love. But perfect love drives out fear, because
fear has to do with punishment. The one who fears is
not made perfect in love," (1 John 4:18 NIV) the fear

that he is referring to is the penalty of wrath one fears from being under the law, but now we have been released from the law (see Rom. 4:14-15, 7:6). The devil has been stripped of his power. His power has been broken because he used the law to condemn us. He took advantage, and still tries to use the opportunity afforded him by the weakness of our flesh, to accuse us every time we fail, but we have been released from the law and the condemnation we suffered while under the law, for Scripture refers to the Old Covenant law as the ministration [or ministry] of death, written and engraven on stones. Further on, it is referred to as the ministration of condemnation (see 2 Cor. 3:6-12).

### *Purpose of the Law*

One could ask, why then was the law given? The Apostle Paul said to the Galatians, "Wherefore the law was our schoolmaster to bring us unto Christ, that we might be justified by faith. But after that faith is come, we are no longer under a schoolmaster." (Gal. 3:24-25)

We are to realize through our failed and futile attempts that we have no hope of trying to gain a righteousness by keeping the law perfectly, and must realize that our only hope is to place our trust in Christ.

The Old Covenant Hebrews who came out of Egypt agreed with God to keep the Covenant of law. When they answered together as a people and said, "All that the Lord hath spoken we will do," (see Ex. 19:7-8), this revealed the pride that was in their hearts, and shortly after they made this declaration, God gave them the Ten Commandments; but they couldn't keep them and neither can we, and our only hope is to place our faith and trust in Christ. When one does, when one becomes born again and passes from death to life, from darkness to light, he or she becomes a new creation (see 2 Cor. 5:17).

### We No Longer Have a Sin Problem

We died to who we once were; we're not who we used to be! But you might be saying, "I am born again, but I don't remember that happening. When did that happen?" That's why the Apostle Paul says in the sixth chapter of Romans, "Don't you know?" (See Rom. 6:3) That means you may not know. He says, in verses 3-7:

> Or don't you know that all of us who were baptized into Christ Jesus were baptized into His death? We were therefore buried with Him through baptism into death in order that just as Christ was raised from the dead through the glory of the Father, we too may live **a new life**. If we have been united with Him like this in His death, we will certainly also be united with Him in His resurrection. For we know that **our old self was crucified with Him**, so that the body of sin might be done away with, that we should no longer be slaves to sin – because anyone who has died has been

*freed from sin.* (Rom. 6:3-7 NIV, emphasis mine)

Now let me ask you. How many of you remember dying? You did when you became born again. You died to your old self, the flesh, and you became spiritually born again. Now let me ask you… can a dead man sin? Can a dead man have guilt? So now we are dead to sin and alive to God. You are dead indeed to what? Sin. Are you worried about your sin problem?

You shouldn't be. It's been done away with.

The Apostle Paul said, "If you have the Spirit, you're not under the law," because you don't need the law if you've already been **made righteous**, so we don't need a law system to make ourselves righteous. This is what happened to us when we became born again. My spirit man, the real me, has been *made righteous*. That's the power of the gospel. I'm not who I used to be and neither are you, if you're born again. You have a new identity. We are now worthy because of what Christ has done. This is all made possible because of the New Covenant.

God said,

> "For this is the covenant that I will make with the house of Israel after those days, saith the Lord; I will put my laws into their mind, and write them in their hearts: and I will be to them a God, and they shall be to me a people: And they shall not teach every man his neighbor, and every man his

> brother, saying, 'Know the Lord'; for all
> shall know me, from the least to the great-
> est. For I will be merciful to their unrigh-
> teousness, and *their sins and their iniquities*
> *will I remember no more.* (Heb. 8:10-12,
> italics mine)

This is God's work of restoration spoken of by the Apostle Paul in his second letter to the Corinthians:

> But all things are from God, Who through
> Jesus Christ reconciled us to Himself [re-
> ceived us into favor, brought us into har-
> mony with Himself] and gave to us the
> ministry of reconciliation [that by word
> and deed we might aim to bring others
> into harmony with Him]. It was God [per-
> sonally present] in Christ, reconciling and
> restoring the world to favor with Himself,
> not counting up and holding against [men]
> their trespasses [but cancelling them] and
> committing to us the message of reconcili-
> ation (of the restoration to favor.) (2 Cor.
> 5:18-19 AMP)

So now, I'll refer back to the Scripture I referenced at the beginning of the chapter,

> Now **we**, brethren, as Isaac was, **are the**
> **children of promise**, but as then, he that
> was born after the flesh persecuted him
> that was born after the Spirit, even so it is
> now. Nevertheless what saith the scripture?

CAST OUT THE BOND WOMAN
AND HER SON: FOR THE SON OF
THE BOND WOMAN SHALL NOT
BE HEIR WITH THE SON OF THE
FREE WOMAN. So then, brethren, we
are not children of the bondwoman, but
of the free. STAND fast therefore in the
liberty wherewith Christ hath made us
free, and be not entangled again with the
yoke of bondage. (Gal. 4:28-5:1, emphasis
mine)

### *Stand Fast*

We are told to **cast out** the bond woman and her son,
and to stand fast in the liberty wherewith Christ hath
made us free and be not entangled again with the yoke
of bondage. The word "liberty" in the Greek carries
the meaning "exempt from liability." We are no longer
under the burden of the law.

This is the same *yoke* referred to by the Apostle Peter
when he stood up and addressed a group of apostles
and elders. We find it in the book of Acts:

But there rose up certain of the sect of the
Pharisees which believed, saying, That it
was needful to circumcise them, and to
command *them* to keep the law of Moses,
And the apostles and elders came together
for to consider of this matter. And when
there had been much disputing, Peter rose
up, and said unto them, Men and brethren,

ye know how that a good while ago God
made choice among us, that the Gentiles
by my mouth should hear the word of
the gospel, and believe. And God, which
knoweth the hearts, bare them witness,
giving them the Holy Ghost, even as he
did *unto us*; And put no difference between
us and them, purifying their hearts by
faith. Now therefore why tempt ye God,
to put a *yoke* upon the neck of the disciples,
which neither our fathers nor we were able
to bear? But we believe that through the
grace of the Lord Jesus Christ we shall be
saved, even as they. (Acts 15:5-11 'yoke'
italics mine)

Once again, "Stand fast therefore in the liberty
wherewith Christ hath made us free, and be not entangled again with the yoke of bondage." (Gal. 5:1)
The phrase "stand fast" is a military term used by Paul
in reference to how we are to **guard the liberty** we
now have in Christ. Paul uses a military term because
we are in for fierce battles that will try to come against
our liberty, but just **where do these battles take place**
and **how are they fought**? What forces come against
our liberty and in what fashion?

Anyone at war must understand his enemy's tactics,
and we are most certainly at war. Not with God, because thanks to the cross *we are at peace with God* (see
Eph. 2:14-15, Rom. 5:1). The enemy is, of course, the
devil. He is a defeated foe, and he has been stripped of

his power. He can no longer use the law against us, for Jesus took it away, nailing it to the cross.

The book of Revelation tells us of a war fought in heaven:

> And there was war in heaven: Michael and his angels fought against the dragon; and the dragon fought and his angels, And prevailed not; neither was their place found any more in heaven. And the great dragon was cast out, that old serpent, called the devil, and satan, which **deceiveth** the whole world: he was cast out into the earth, and his angels were cast out with him. (Rev. 12:7-9, emphasis mine)

Approximately one third of the angels fell with satan. Satan is called the accuser of the brethren. He and his fallen cohorts try to put condemnation on people by using the law. He's a master legalist and he and they try to **deceive** anyone who falls prey, anyone who doesn't know [or stand on] the liberty we have in Christ. Paul talks of this war we wage in the second book of Corinthians.

> For though we walk in the flesh, we do not war after the flesh: (For the weapons of our warfare are not carnal, but mighty through God to the pulling down of strong holds;) **Casting down imaginations**, and every high thing that exalteth itself against the knowledge of God, and bringing into

captivity *every thought* to the obedience of
Christ. (2 Cor. 10:3-5, empahsis mine)

### *Cast Out the Lie ~ Embrace the Truth*

By now I hope with what we've covered so far you
have an understanding of the love and acceptance God
has for **you** and for me, and has demonstrated to us by
sending His Son Jesus to die for us. The truth of what
Christ has done will stand for all eternity. But we have
an enemy who is on a smear campaign to discredit
God's good name, nature, and the love that embodies
who He is. The Apostle John wrote, "The thief cometh
not, but for to steal, and to kill, and to destroy: I am
come that they might have life, and that they might
have *it* more abundantly." (John 10:10)

God says through the prophet Jeremiah, "For I
know the thoughts that I think toward you, saith the
LORD, thoughts of peace, and not of evil, to give you
an expected end." (Jer. 29:11)

God is truly for us and any thought or imagination
contrary to this truth, we must choose to reject. The
Apostle Paul said in his epistle to the Ephesians, "His
intent was that now, through the church, the manifold
wisdom of God should be made known to the rulers
and authorities in the heavenly realms, according to
his eternal purpose that he accomplished in Christ Jesus our Lord." (Eph. 3:10-11 NIV)

This is saying that we, as born again believers, are
to use our God-given authority in the name of Christ,

from whom we have been given the legal right to use it, and make it known to the fallen angels that are in the heavenly realms that we have authority over them (see Eph. 6:10-18). We cast down any lie that doesn't line up with the truth. The enemy tries to come against *our worth*, but remember, we are **new creations** and seen worthy by God. We are justified and made righteous and we are free from all condemning lies that the enemy would try to get us to believe.

Paul spent the first six chapters of Romans framing these very truths, and then brings us to chapter seven, which seems strangely out of place. At first he gives an illustration from marriage about how we died to the law. He then goes into explaining a struggle with sin, and climaxes the chapter by saying,

> So I find this law at work: Although I want to do good, evil is right there with me. For in my inner being I delight in God's law, But I see another law at work in me, waging war against the law of my mind and making me a prisoner of the law of sin at work within me. What a wretched man I am! Who will rescue me from this body that is subject to death? Thanks be to God, who delivers me through Jesus Christ our Lord! So then, I myself in my mind am a slave to God's law, but in my sinful nature a slave to the law of sin. (Rom. 7:21-25 NIV)

What is the Apostle Paul talking about when he

says, "But I see another law at work in me, waging war against the law of my mind and making me a prisoner of the law of sin at work within me."? (Rom. 7:23 NIV) I've heard some say, "Well, Paul battled with doubts just as do many others," but that would have left Paul a pretty sad, un-victorious Christian; somewhat of a victim; quite a contradiction from the one God used to pen three-fourths of the New Testament and who said, "I can do all things through Christ which strengtheneth me." (Phil. 4:13)

No, the war that the Apostle Paul is speaking of here is the war taking place within every person, Christian and unbeliever.

## *The War of Flesh vs. Spirit*

This is the war that the flesh has with the Spirit, spoken of in Galatians: "For the flesh desires what is contrary to the Spirit, and the Spirit what is contrary to the flesh. They are in conflict with each other, so that you are not to do whatever you want." (Gal. 5:17 NIV)

The King James Version of Galatians 5:17, reads as follows: "For the flesh lusteth against the Spirit, and the Spirit against the flesh: and these are contrary the one to the other: so that ye cannot do the things that ye would."

What is taking place here between the flesh and the Spirit that makes them contrary, the one to the other? They're not in agreement and never will be. Are they contrary to each other because the flesh wants us to do all sorts of evil things, such as steal, kill, slander, gossip, boast, lie, etc. and the Spirit wants us to go to church, help people, give money to the needy, read the Bible, pray, and join a church, etc.? After all, the one seems so right and the other so wrong. The reason the flesh lusts against the Spirit and the Spirit against the flesh is that the flesh wants us to try and *gain a righteousness by our own effort*. The flesh thinks it can do it on its own, but the Spirit says the only way you'll ever be righteous or gain the righteousness of God is by putting your faith in Christ, by becoming born again.

Now once you become born again and receive a new Spirit with a new nature and a new heart, your desires change, especially as you **renew your mind** to who you [now] are. God said, concerning the New Covenant, that He would write His laws on our hearts. So now, we are led from within, by the leading and prompting of the Holy Spirit, not by an external code of laws. But, as a Christian, if you put yourself *back under the law*, you are bringing yourself back under the ministry of condemnation and death (see 2 Cor. 3:7-9).

That's why the Apostle Paul said, in the seventh chapter of Romans, "Who will rescue me from this body that is subject to death?" (Rom. 7:24b NIV) But then, his answer is found in the first verse of Romans chapter eight,

> Therefore, there is now no condemnation
> for those who are in Christ Jesus, because
> through Christ Jesus the law of **the Spirit**

> **who gives life** has set you free from the
> law of sin and death. For what the law was
> powerless to do because it was weakened
> by the flesh - God did by sending his own
> Son in the likeness of sinful flesh to be a sin
> offering. And so he condemned sin in the
> flesh, in order that the righteous require-
> ment of the law might be fully met in us,
> who do not live according to the flesh but
> according to the Spirit. (Rom. 8:1-4 NIV,
> emphasis mine)

Looking at these verses found earlier in chapter sev-
en of Romans, we read,

> So, my brothers and sisters, you also died
> to the law through the body of Christ that
> you might *belong to another*, to Him who
> was raised from the dead, in order that we
> might bear fruit for God. For when we
> were in the realm of the flesh, the sinful
> passions aroused by the law were at work
> in us, so that we bore fruit for death. But
> now, by dying to what once bound us, we
> have been **released from the law** so that we
> serve in the new way of the Spirit, and not
> in the old way of the written code. (Rom.
> 7:4-6 NIV, emphasis mine)

When you place yourself under the law as a Christian, you come under the condemnation of the law. As
a Christian, you still remain the righteousness of God

and you continue to be in right-standing with God, but *in your mind* you are taking on this condemnation. Scripture says, "For when we were in the realm of the flesh, the sinful passions aroused by the law were at work in us, so that we bore fruit for death." (Rom. 7:5 NIV-UK)

### *Sin is Strengthened by the Law*

How is it that sinful passions are aroused by the law? Why is it that if you tell someone not to do something, often that thing you told them not to do is just about all they can think about? So we can see, when a Christian places himself under the law, he is putting himself in the realm of the flesh [in his thinking] – the flesh says I can do it on my own. I can be righteous apart from God. When one, as a Christian, takes himself out from under the law, he is removing himself from the realm of the flesh [in his thinking] and is now operating [in his thinking, and remember that actions follow thoughts] in the realm of the Spirit. He is operating, or you could say, he is controlled by the Spirit. Remember, the Spirit says that the only way you'll ever be righteous is not by the law, but by what Jesus did when he fulfilled the law. This is the righteousness you gained unconditionally when you became born again... *the righteousness you received as a free gift.*

### *No More Condemnation*

A great example of this is something I've seen many

times. Christians who smoke often feel very con-
demned. Some I've known have allowed this condemnation to hinder them from church attendance and
fellowship. They feel beat up with condemnation because of their powerlessness to quit this habit, but if
they are born again, are they righteous? Yes, they are,
and they have to know that they are and rest in this
*truth*. Righteousness means they have a right-standing
with God, apart from their works or self-effort. Now,
we know smoking is harmful, and God knows it too,
but this addictive habit is very difficult to break. If
a Christian who smokes rests in the fact that he or
she is in right-standing with God, *even as a smoker*, he
removes himself from the condemnation of the law,
along with the desires or sinful passions *aroused by the
law*, and thus eventually loses the desire to smoke,
breaking his dependency on this habit. God wasn't
mad at him for smoking. He's the One who made a
way to set him free.

The enemy is on a smear campaign to distort our
view of God's true love for us. It says in the book of
Colossians, "And you, that were sometime alienated
and enemies *in your mind* by wicked works, yet now
hath He reconciled in the body of his flesh through
death, to present you holy and unblameable and unre-
proveable in His sight;" (Col. 1:21-22).

The world tries to conform us into believing many
lies which come against the truth of who we are as born-
again Christians. Many voices speak at us through the
media and many other sources, all trying to vie for our

attention and shape our opinion of how we view ourselves. The TV commercials scream the message that unless you are a young woman or girl with a "Barbie doll figure" you don't measure up somehow, when in fact God looks at you with the eyes of love and says, "You are accepted in the Beloved, I made you and nothing shall separate you from My love." (See Rom. 8:35). "I formed you in your mother's womb, you are fearfully and wonderfully made and you are My child." (See Jer. 1:5, Ps. 139)

### *The Culture and our Emotions*

The ever-changing culture, a number of decades ago, would have acknowledged that marriage is between a man and a woman, and now wants to tell us that marriage is not solely between a man and a woman, even though God's Word clearly says that it is. How does a person find the truth? How does a person know the will of God? It's mainly by going to the Word of God (see Rom. 12:1-2). Jesus said in the gospel of John, "The Spirit gives life; the flesh counts for nothing. The words I have spoken to you are Spirit and they are life." (John 6:63 NIV) It also says in John; "Sanctify them by Your truth. Your word is truth." (John 17:17 NKJV)

What we allow to come in through our eye gates and ear gates, or we receive through circumstances which have influenced our thinking and emotions, must all be filtered through the Word of God.

Take for example a person who has had a traumatic event happen to them. For that person, that topic will be more emotionally charged than it would be for a person who hadn't actually experienced the same trauma. A person (child or young adult) whose parents have gone through a divorce may find it difficult to relate to God as a loving Father. A woman who has been the victim of rape or abuse by a man may find it difficult to enter into marriage and trust a man in a manner that would allow for a healthy marriage relationship.

A man who was brought up under a tyrannical parent may in turn allow the harsh leadership under which he was raised to enter into his marriage relationship and influence the way he treats his wife. The manner in which we were raised and lived before coming to Christ has greatly influenced the way we think, *but we are not victims.*

### *Freedom For All*

When the Apostle Paul said in his first letter to the Corinthians,

> Each one should remain in the situation which he was in when God called him. Were you a slave when you were called? Don't let it trouble you – although if you can gain your freedom, do so. For he who was a slave when he was called by the Lord is the Lord's freed man; similarly, he who was a free man when he was called is

Christ's slave. You were bought at a price;
do not become slaves of men. Brothers,
each man, as responsible to God, should
remain in the situation God called him to.
(1 Cor. 7:20-24 NIV)

He was not advocating slavery.

What Paul meant when he said this was not as some
now accuse Paul of saying, which is… "Paul must have
condoned slavery." We can even see from verse 21 that
Paul said, "Were you a slave when you were called?
Don't let it trouble you – although if you can gain
your freedom, do so."

Although the Apostle Paul didn't agree with slavery,
he recognized that slavery was a part of the society in
which they lived. In fact, Israel was under Roman oc-
cupation or rule. The Jewish Old Covenant law found
in the book of Leviticus lists the laws given regard-
ing intendured servants. For a deeper understanding
of slavery in this time period, I recommend googling
"Slavery under Israel's Levitical priesthood." I don't
believe the Apostle Paul wanted any man to be a slave.
Once again, he said, "If you can gain your freedom
do so," but that was just the point… some could not.
This is how it was at that time…..and then along came
the Apostle Paul and others preaching from city to
city, speaking of the freedom we have in Christ and
telling the people that all you have to do is put your
faith in Christ and know the truth and the truth will
set you free, which is all true. But what if you had been
a slave, a prisoner or a thief hanging on the cross next

to Jesus, and heard this message? Well, that's exactly the point Paul was making. This freedom is available to all. Some of the "most free" people in the world are sitting in jail cells and some of the most imprisoned people are walking the streets, imprisoned by fears, hopelessness, lies, and in bondage to desires that rule their bodies and souls.

They can be released from these. The culture we live in today wants to say that homosexuality is a "born desire." But the Word of God tells us that desires for the same sex are a perversion of natural desires (see Rom. 1:20). People can be released from any perversion of the truth, but one needs to recognize the truth. *The gospel of God's grace and His unconditional love and acceptance is the truth that the enemy is trying to twist and distort any way he can.*

### *We Are One With Jesus*

When Satan was kicked out of heaven, he took approximately a third of the angels with him. Now, all he and his cohorts can do is lie and come against the truth of the plan that God had from the foundation of the world. If you listen to these lies, you are allowing him to play you like a puppet. You may have come from a dysfunctional home, or been born with an ailment, but remember Jesus said, "The thief comes only to steal and kill and destroy; I have come *that they may have life*, and have it to the full." (John 10:10 NIV)

Don't agree with the devil and lie against the truth

(see James 3:14b-15). Once again, the book of Romans states, "The word is near you; it is in your mouth and in your heart, that is, the word of faith we are proclaiming." (Rom. 10:8 NIV)

We gain salvation through confessing with our mouth and believing in our heart. That's how we became born again, new creations, given new life. Now that we are new creations, we may look and find ourselves in the same body or the same situation. But *Jesus became sin for us.* He was beaten with stripes on His back for our healing. He died for our sin and rose to newness of life, and spiritually speaking, we are seated with him in the heavenlies; we've been raised with Him (see Eph. 2:6). We are also one Spirit with Him (see 1 Cor. 6:17).

You may be saying, "I don't remember that happening, besides I'm here in my room, or in a wheelchair," but if you're born again, **it did happen**. We're seated with Christ in the heavenlies.

This word "seated" refers to authority, just as the county **seat** is the place of authority for your county.

And now, as born-again Christians, the Word of God says, "Yet to all who received Him, to those who believed in His name, He gave the right to become children of God - **children born not of natural descent**, nor of human decision, or a husband's will, but born of God," (John 1:12-13 NIV)

This means we are **one with Christ**; we have God's Name and the legal right to use it. So now we stand in our authority and claim the promises of God that are freely given us (see 2 Cor. 4:13). Remember Scripture says, "…as He is so are we in this world." (1 John 4:17b)

Does Jesus now have sin?  No. Is Jesus sick? No. Is Jesus mentally disturbed or depressed? No. Is Jesus poor? No. Jesus is more alive than ever and so are we. Let's know and believe the truth in our hearts and confess with our mouths.

The book of Proverbs says, "Keep thy heart with all diligence; for out of it are the issues of life." (Prov. 4:23) Jesus said, "A good man out of the good treasure of his heart bringeth forth that which is good; and an evil man out of the evil treasure of his heart bringeth forth that which is evil: for of the abundance of the heart his mouth speaketh.  And why call ye me, Lord, Lord, and do not the things which I say?" (Luke 6:45-46)

We as Christians have new hearts that are not evil hearts (see Ez. 11:19). We are *one with Christ* and He doesn't have an evil heart. We know the gospel, which is **good news**, and we know God's heart is **for** us. We can *guard the gates of our heart* by resting in Christ's finished work, which is proclaimed in the Word of God.

### *Reject the Lies of the Enemy*

We find in the book of Amos; "Hate the evil and love the good, and *establish judgment in the gate*: it may be that the Lord God of hosts will be gracious unto the remnant of Joseph." (Amos 5:15, italics mine)

God is a **good** God who is not holding our sin against us. We must *reject any lies* to the contrary. The Apostle Paul wrote in his second letter to the Corinthians about how we are to wage war against the lies of the enemy. He said,

> For though we walk in the flesh, we do not war after the flesh: (for the weapons of our warfare are not carnal, but mighty through God to the pulling down of strongholds) Casting down imaginations and every high thing that exalteth itself against the knowledge of God, and bringing into captivity **every thought** to the obedience of Christ; And having in a readiness to revenge all disobedience, when your obedience is fulfilled." (2 Cor. 10:3-6. See also Rom. 1:5)

The strongholds that are to be pulled down are the formations of thoughts, thought patterns, or mindsets that run contrary to the *truth of God*. Remember, before you were born again you were on a fast track heading down the highway of life. You were trying to *earn your way* to heaven by your effort and performance.

### *We Must Man the Gates*

Then you heard the truth of the gospel, the message that said it wasn't your performance, but what Christ did on the cross that offered you His *unconditional* pardon, and you accepted His offer. He took your sin and gave you His righteousness. You accepted His sacrificial atonement. You repented, which means you changed the direction of your thinking; you went in the other direction.

Now, you are the righteousness of God in Christ Jesus, all because of Jesus. So every time a thought enters your mind that is contrary to this truth, you must recognize it and choose to reject it. You must man **the gate**. Failure to do so allows the enemy access into your mind. The enemy wants to enter our minds so he can gain access to our hearts, but it's **our responsibility** to stop the lies of the enemy. Also, the Apostle Paul said, when we do this, we are casting down imaginations and high things that exalt themselves against the knowledge of God. These high things and imaginations are the lies that try to cover up the truth of what Jesus has done.

But we must cast the lies down; reject them. We are the ones who *man the gate* and choose what to let in and what to keep out. Your parents might not believe in God, but you can. Your pastor might not believe healing is for today, but you can know that it is. It's up to you to dig in to the Word of God and find and hold on to the truth. As we gain truth, we must be patient with people and understand there is a learning curve. We are to be gentle when we instruct (see 2 Tim. 2:25).

It's interesting to examine the word "gate" and where and how it is used in the Bible. Concerning the

Bible, there is something called the "law of first mention", which means this was the first time a particular word was used in Scripture, thus giving it its deepest meaning.

Well, if you read Dr. Walter Zorn's review of **Ancient City Gates** later in this book, he makes the statement that in the Hebrew Bible the word "gate" (sha'ar) is used c. 375 times (for "gates" of cities, towns, palaces, temples, private houses, etc.) [A couple of synonyms are used rarely, "gate" or "opening" for petach and "gate" or "door" for deleth.] I wish to focus on the last synonym used here which is "door".

### *Agree with God*

Do you know where the word "door" shows up for the first time in the Bible? You may have guessed it. It's found in the fourth chapter of Genesis and reads:

> The Lord looked with favor on Abel and his offering but on Cain and his offering he did not look with favor. So Cain was very angry, and his face was downcast. Then the Lord said to Cain, Why are you angry? Why is your face downcast? If you do what is right, will you not be accepted? But if you do not do what is right, sin is crouching **at your door**; it desires to have you, but you must master it. (Gen. 4:4b-7 NIV, highlights mine)

Notice it says, "The Lord looked with favor on Abel

and his offering but on Cain and his offering he did not look with favor."

What was it about their offerings that caused God to look with favor upon one and not the other? Gen. 4:3 tells us, "In the course of time Cain brought some of the fruits of the soil as an offering to the Lord but Abel brought fat portions from some of the first born of his flock." (Gen. 4:3-4a NIV) What was different about the two offerings was that Cain brought an offering of some of the fruit he had grown, but Abel brought fat portions from some of the first born of his flock.

For Abel to do this he obviously had to kill the animal(s) and shed the blood. Remember Leviticus 17:11 and Hebrews 9:22 tell us, "without the shedding of blood there is no forgiveness of sin." Both Abel and his offering were accepted by God. Cain was downcast and angry, but God said, "If you do what is right, will you not be accepted?" Now when was the first animal sacrifice done... and by whom? Well, it was done by God Himself when he killed the animals with which to cover Adam and Eve. This is really something.

And then I thought about another well-known Scripture towards the end of the Bible. It's not at the end of the book of Revelation, but it's near the end of what Jesus told the Apostle John to write in his letters to the seven churches. It's found in Revelation 3:20 and reads; "Behold, I stand at the door and knock: if any man hear my voice, **and open the door**, I will come in to him, and will sup with him, and he with me." God offers his invitation to everlasting life and we now must show people the "message of this new life" (see Acts 5:20b). But let's not just give them the message. Let's also get involved in their lives.

I believe the saying is true that people don't care how much you know until they know how much you care. It's not enough to hand someone a book and say, "Here, read this." The Pharisee in the Good Samaritan story, told by Jesus, sidestepped a person who needed help because he was afraid of being defiled by coming in contact with that person. He was worried about his sin problem. We don't have to worry about that, so we can truly help people.

Remember earlier in this book, I said the word "wicked" is derived from the word "wicker" because wicker is twisted. Well, now [you] as a Christian...are found righteous – made straight, and you can choose to end the war in your mind and think thoughts that *agree with God.*

I'll end this chapter with a verse found in Isaiah, "Let the wicked forsake his way, and the unrighteous man his thoughts: and let him return unto the Lord, and he will have mercy upon him; and to our God, for he will abundantly pardon." (Isa. 55:7)

# TWO

## The Gates

In the first chapter we discussed many things, the new life we receive as Christians and the fact that we as believers no longer have the wrath of God abiding on us. These are major chords of truth expressed in the Word which give us great cause for joy. Another truth we examined is the fact that we, apart from Christ, didn't and couldn't attain the righteousness of God on our own merit or human effort. Our sin problem and our condition of being spiritually dead, were remedied by Christ's death and resurrection. For as stated in 1 John 1:9, "If we confess our sins, He is faithful and just to forgive us our sins, and to cleanse us from ALL unrighteousness." (Emphasis mine) And that is just what God does when you repent. (Remember, to repent means to change direction; to change your thinking and to go the other way), which is what you did when you became born again.

Before you were born again, you in effect, were saying you could gain a righteousness on your own, with your own effort and performance. Then you heard the *gospel of grace* and you learned of a righteousness apart from works, all because of what Jesus did. You changed direction in your thinking and put your faith in God and not in yourself. This was true repentance and you received the righteousness of God; a free gift. This is what happened to you if you became a born-again Christian.

### *Forgotten That They Were Cleansed*

But then, you went to church and they said, "You must walk a tightrope and not fail in any areas and if you do, you must '1st John 1:9 it,'" which left you continually keeping a short list of your behavior. You became introspective and never really felt like you had a clear, guilt-free conscience… and it's no wonder because you failed to remember that you died to sin (see Rom. 6:3). You also lost sight of what Christ did in His work of reconciliation.

As Paul states in his second epistle to the Corinthians, "Now all things are of God, who has reconciled us to Himself through Jesus Christ, and has given us the ministry of reconciliation. That is that God was in Christ reconciling the world to himself, **not imputing their trespasses to them**, and has committed to us the word of reconciliation." (2 Cor. 5:18-19 NKJV) (See also Hebrews 8:10-12) So even though you may have failed in an area, you still remain the righteousness of God. You don't bounce from light to darkness and then back to light upon your confession of your failure.

### *The Need to Restore One Another*

Some people might tell you that the Bible says you need to examine yourself. The only time God tells us to examine ourselves is to know if we are *in the faith,* not to search ourselves for sin (see 2 Cor. 13:5). In Scripture, it says to confess one to another, but for this to truly happen as it should in the church, one has to know he's not being judged of God or by the people in his church (see Rom. 8:1). That's what gives us the freedom to believe we will truly receive help in the areas we need it.

God's love is truly unconditional. Through the finished work of the cross, God has made a way for all to come to Him. We all fail in many ways, even as believers, but Christ is our perfect High Priest who will never fail us or accuse us. As God's word states, "There is therefore now no condemnation to them which are in Christ Jesus." (Rom. 8:1)

Then why and to whom was 1 John 1:9 written? To quote another minister of the gospel:

> When Paul and Peter penned their letters, they were writing to a Christian pastor who was to read them to a congregation of people made up of both lost and saved, like our congregations of today. The saved are built up in their faith, and the lost have the opportunity to see their need for salvation and come to faith in Jesus Christ.

> Reading 1 John 1:9 in context, we see that

it is addressing the lost, not the believer. At the time John wrote this letter, about 90 AD, a heretical group, which was a forerunner of the Gnostics, was teaching that mankind is without sin. Today we still find these doctrines taught through such groups as the Christian Scientists and other metaphysical "churches." The Gnostics believed that all matter is evil and only spirit is good, therefore, they said Jesus couldn't have come in the flesh, because flesh is matter. So they concluded that Jesus was just an illusion.

Now, let me ask you, if Jesus did not come in the flesh, what happens to the gospel message? If He did not die physically, we are still under the condemnation of sin and death. If He was not raised up physically, we are still spiritually dead, separated from the life of Christ. So, to deny that Jesus came in the flesh is to deny the gospel.

John was addressing this issue in his first letter. Notice how he begins: "That which was from the beginning, which we have heard, which we have seen with our own eyes, which we have looked at and our hands have touched – this we proclaim concerning the word of life." (1 John 1:1) Why do you suppose John began his letter this way? It was to dispel the Gnostic heresy that was making the rounds in the churches in those days. The Gnostics also believed that man didn't have a sin nature. And even if he did, it didn't matter. John addressed this heresy in verse 8 and 10 of 1 John 1. We quote 1 John 1:9 so often, but we seldom look at what is said in the verses before and after: "If we claim to be without sin, we deceive ourselves and the truth is not in us. If we claim we have not sinned, we make Him out to be a liar, and his word has no place in our lives." What John wrote in his second letter clarifies that this is a passage to unbelievers: "To the chosen lady and her children, whom I love in the truth – and not I only, but also all who know the truth – because of the truth which lives in us and will be with us forever." (2 John 1-2)

Compare this with 1 John 1:8, which says, "If we claim to be without sin, we deceive ourselves, and the truth is not in us." If the truth lives in us and will be with us forever, can believers ever say that the truth is not in them? This would be double-talk. How can these two verses both be referring to Christians? The only conclusion we can make is that those in 1 John 1:8, who claim to be without sin, are lost and are later referred to as antichrists.[1]

---

1    Taken from "What About 1 John 1:9?" by Bob George, pages 14-17 Used with permission by Bob George, People to People Ministries

### Rest in Christ

Thank God for people who have these insights. Now we know that we don't always have to be searching ourselves or examining our faults. We can rest—knowing that we are "the righteousness of God in Christ Jesus." Some may say this is license to sin or fail. Well, the truth is, if we do come short, God is not judging us as Christians, but there are still consequences [for sin] here on earth.

If I were to speed through a crowded area of traffic, I could cause great harm. I could be put in jail, lose my license and be shamed in the eyes of those who know me. There are still consequences [in the earth] for our actions in this sense. But why would I want to do those things and disrespect the freedom that Christ died to bring me.

If a Christian were to seldom read his Bible and spend large amounts of time with the wrong crowd and didn't have his or her mind renewed to who they are in Christ, they could, sad to say, reach such a bad place and be in a situation where they could deny Christ. That would be their own sad choice. But once again, knowing who we are in Christ and knowing the love He has for us and that He desires we share with others, is motivation to allow our lives to be living epistles that speak of God's grace, mercy and love.

### A Righteousness Which is by Faith

Abraham remained the righteousness of God, which he

had obtained through faith. It **was by** faith, for Abraham lived nearly 400 years before the law was given. He remained the righteousness of God, even though he and Sarah conspired to have Ishmael through Sarah's hand maiden, Hagar. This was a work of the flesh that didn't bring about the promise of God. In fact, it had consequences for Abraham and Sarah, as well as far reaching consequences for us today, as we ..sadly, see much of the nation of Israel still being persecuted by many of the descendants of Ishmael.

But Abraham's relationship with God was still intact, he was still righteous, which means he remained in right-standing with God; made straight. So now, you can clearly see the great advantage we have over the Old Covenant saints, because ours is a *better Covenant based on better promises.* (See Heb. 7:22)

The Old Testament saints were under the law and the Levitical priesthood, who saw to the ceremonial animal sacrifices (see Heb. 7:11). If they failed or were led astray through the influence of evil kings or false prophets who spoke lies to the people and failed to properly warn them, they fell to calamity, which affected their borders and the peace of the entire nation of Israel, ultimately causing its divide and the people to go into the banishment of exile (see Zech. 7:11-12, Lam. 2:14).

### *Turn Back the Battle at the Gate*

But, if our battle is in our minds, and theirs was at

their borders or city walls when enemies would threaten their security, what is our response to be and what was theirs? Are there similarities that we can draw, and learn from the mistakes and victories of these Old Covenant people? Let's start to examine these questions by first looking at various Scriptures. The first is found in the book of Isaiah and is a hymn of praise which goes as follows:

> And in THAT day you will say: "OH LORD, I will praise You; Though you were angry with me, Your anger is turned away, and You comfort me. Behold, God is my salvation, I will trust and not be afraid; For YAH, the LORD, is **my strength** and song, He also has become my salvation." Therefore with joy you will draw water From the wells of salvation. (Isa. 12:1-3 NKJV, emphasis mine)

God's anger is turned away and He **does** comfort us. *He is our strength and has become our salvation.* Therefore we can have joy. This is evident by the many Scriptures we have examined from the Word of God thus far.

Now let's look at what God spoke through the prophet Isaiah in chapter 28 saying, "In that day the LORD Almighty will be a glorious crown, a beautiful wreath for the remnant of His people. He will be a spirit of justice to the one who sits in judgment, a source of strength to those **who turn back the battle at the gate.**" (Isa. 28:5-6 NIV, emphasis mine)

The Jewish people who were delivered out of Egypt spent 40 years in their wilderness wanderings. Of the generation that came out of Egypt, only two survived to enter the Promised Land; Joshua and Caleb. It was the second generation for the most part who entered the Promised Land under the leadership of Joshua, who had replaced Moses. God said in Deuteronomy:

> When the Lord your God brings you into the land He swore to your fathers, to Abraham, Isaac and Jacob, to give you – a land with large, flourishing cities you did not build, houses filled with all kinds of good things you did not provide, wells you did not dig, and vineyards and olive groves you did not plant – Then when you eat and are satisfied, be careful that you do not forget the Lord, who brought you out of Egypt, out of the land of slavery. (Deut. 6:10-12 NIV)

Later in the book of Deuteronomy, God said through Moses,

> After the Lord your God has driven them out before you, do not say to yourself, "The LORD has brought me here to take possession of this land because of my righteousness." No, it is on account of the wickedness of these nations that the Lord is going to drive them out before you. It is not because of your righteousness or your integrity that you are going in to take possession of their

land; but on account of the wickedness of these nations, the LORD your God will drive them out before you, to accomplish what he swore to your fathers, to Abraham, Isaac and Jacob. Understand then, that it is not because of your righteousness that the LORD your God is giving you this good land to possess, for you are a stiff necked people. (Deut. 9:4-6 NIV)

God spoke this through Moses not too long before they entered the Promised Land.

In the epistle of Hebrews, it's written that the Holy Spirit says:

Today, if you hear his voice, do not harden your hearts as you did in the rebellion, during the time of testing in the desert, where your fathers tested and tried me, and for forty years saw what I did. That is why I was angry with that generation, and I said, "Their hearts are always going astray, and they have not known my ways." So I declared on oath in my anger, "They shall never enter my rest." (Heb. 3:7b-11 NIV)

### *A Clean Conscience*

These people were under the Covenant of law, if they did good… they got good. If they did bad… they got bad. Scripture tells us that through the law we become conscious of sin (see Rom. 3:20). The word "conscience" means: con [with] - science [knowledge], so these people living under the law were knowledgeable about their sin. It could be said they were sin-conscious and with that came the fear of punishment (see Heb. 2:15). This mentality affected the Hebrew people in the wilderness. It affected them once they crossed over into the Promised Land, and it affects people today, if they *allow themselves* to be put under the law.

The Word of God says, "But now, we are delivered from the law, that being dead wherein we were held; that we should serve in newness of spirit and not in the oldness of the letter." (Rom. 7:6) Once again, I'll repeat Isa. 28:5-6 NIV (emphasis mine), "In that day the LORD Almighty will be a glorious crown, a beautiful wreath for the remnant of his people. He will be a spirit of justice to the one who sits in judgment, a source of strength to those **who turn back the battle at the gate**." When the Hebrews entered the Promised Land and dispossessed other peoples and took over their property and structures, they fortified certain cities with thick walls that were a defense against the attack of enemy intruders who might try to invade their borders and attack their cities.

The Covenant of law was a conditional Covenant and one of the requirements God said they must keep, to be faithful to the Covenant, is found in Exodus, where God said, "Thrice in the year shall all your men-children appear before the LORD GOD, the God of Israel. For I will cast out the nations before thee, and enlarge thy borders: **neither shall any man desire thy**

**land when thou shalt go up to appear before the LORD thy God thrice in the year."** (Ex. 34:23-24, emphasis mine)

With time, this stipulation and others would find the Hebrews unfaithful, and enemies would invade their borders causing death and destruction to those who were caught outside of the walled cities, but those inside the thick walls and heavily built gates found protection; the gates, of course, being the access points into and out of these cities.

The significance of these gates to the Old Testament Hebrews is very profound, and as we shall see, played a major role in many areas of their lives. To further study this we'll read a review written by Dr. Walter D. Zorn entitled *Ancient City Gates*.[2]

## ANCIENT CITY GATES

Ancient city gates are mentioned many times in the Bible, particularly in the Hebrew Bible (Old Testament). But many Bible students do not understand their use or importance in terms of ancient culture and the history of Israel. The following is a short but significant review of the several usages of ancient city gates which will give us insight into the biblical text.

In the Hebrew Bible the word "gate" (*sha'ar*) is used c. 375 times (for "gates" of cities, towns,

---

2        Used in its entirety with permission by Dr. Walter D. Zorn, Lincoln Christian University

palaces, temples, private houses, etc.). [A couple of synonyms are used rarely, "gate" or "opening" for *petach* and "gate" or "door" for *deleth*.] Thus, we have no lack of biblical references to help us understand the importance and usages of ancient city gates. Also, archaeological excavations of ancient city sites almost always find a "city gate or gates" with which to work (at least the foundations).

Ancient cities protected themselves by means of strong, mammoth walls which included one or more gates. These city gates became the focus of enemies as the "weak spots" of a city's defenses. Thus, city planners and builders created increasingly more and more complex gate systems to protect the city and its walls. But defense was only a small part of ancient city gate usages. As Ray Vander Laan summarized:

The gate was the center of city life in biblical times. Originally designed to defend a city against attack, this massive structure soon became a combination of community center, city hall, and marketplace. People paid their taxes in the city gate, and officials settled legal matters there. Prophets prophesied and kings ruled in the gate. Shops and markets around the gate provided for the people's daily needs. Lot sat in the gate of Sodom. In the gate, Boaz established his legal right to marry Ruth. Absalom won the affection of Israel in the gate. The Bible predicts the return of the Messiah for the Last Judgment in the symbolism of the Eastern Gate of Jerusalem. When we understand these complex structures, we have a "window" on life in biblical times. (*That The World May Know*. Teacher's Guide I, p. 14.)

It is difficult to imagine how in ancient times one area could be used in such a variety of ways, equivalent to our modern-day armory, courthouse, city hall, open-air preaching meetings, malls and market area, political conventions, daily news "paper," and general community center. Let's look at some biblical and archaeological sources to help us understand this phenomenon in some organized fashion.

## I. Defensive Purposes

The primary purpose of the ancient city gates was to have controlled access to a walled city. The "gates" were usually double wooden doors (Neh 2:3, 17), often plated with metal (Ps 107:16; Isa 45:2), secured with an iron bar (1 Kgs 4:13; Ps. 107:16) or even wooden bar (Nahum 3:13). (See also Deut 3:5 and 2 Chron 8:5; 14:7.) Usually cities had one main gate (Jerusalem had ten gates and Ezekiel's idealized city had 12 gates). In most cities there was an outer and inner gate (2 Sam 18:24). By Solomon's time gates were more complex. Solomon had three cities fortified (1 Kgs 9:15) to protect the main trade route, the Via Maris: Hazor, Megiddo, and Gezer. Excavations at these ancient cities have revealed the so-called "Solomonic" gate complex: three pairs of long narrow piers separated by two pairs of long narrow recesses and resembling the 10th century B.C. gateways at Charchemish. The enclosed rooms at the sides of the gates were primarily for guards and military supplies (2 Sam 18:24 – "room above the gate"). Huge towers on either side of the gate complex (2 Chron 26:9; 2 Sam 18:24; 18:33) enabled soldiers to see approaching enemies from a distance and, of course, were the place for the gate watchmen. The watchmen closed the gates at night (Josh 2:5; Neh 7:3).Even if an enemy could break through the outer gates (double doors), they would be confronted on three sides by soldiers who could attack from above or drop down into the battle below—in three different areas! And even then another "inner gate" would have to be negotiated before the city itself could be reached. While these gate complexes were formidable to break or burn down, they could be destroyed with persistence. However, it is interesting to note how often ancient armies resorted to sieges and simply starved the citizens out!

The biblical literature and ways of talking about war included the city gates. Note the following references. Ezekiel describes how Jerusalem's gates were attacked by the Babylonians: "I have stationed the sword for slaughter at all their gates. ...to set battering rams against the gates, to build a ramp and to erect siege works" (Ezek 21:15, 22). Earlier Deut 28:52ff. had warned about this: "They will lay siege to all the cities throughout your land until the high fortified walls in which you trust fall down. They will besiege all the cities throughout the land the LORD your God is giving you." "**To possess the gate" was to possess the city** (Gen 22:17; 24:60). Deborah's sarcastic victory poem reprimands: "When they chose new gods, war came to the city gates... . Then the people of the LORD went down to the city gates" (Judg 5:8, 11).

In several oracles Isaiah proclaims: "The gates of Zion will lament and mourn; destitute, she will sit on the ground" (3:26); "Your choicest valleys are full of chariots, and horsemen are posted at the city gates; the defenses of Judah are stripped away" (22:7-8a); "The city is left in ruins, its gate is battered to pieces" (24:12); and "He will be a spirit of justice to him who sits in judgment, a source of strength to those who turn back the battle at the gate" (28:6). When the people are disobedient to the laws of God, Jeremiah cries out on behalf of God: "I will kindle an unquenchable fire in the gates of Jerusalem that will consume her fortresses" (17:27b). Ironically, Jeremiah warns the Babylonians: "Babylon's thick wall will be leveled and her high gates set on fire" (51:58a). Jeremiah finally laments: "All her gateways [i.e., Jerusalem's] are desolate" (Lam 1:4b). Eyewitnesses reported to Nehemiah: "The wall of Jerusalem is broken down, and its gates have been burned with fire" (Neh 1:3b). So while ancient city gates were primarily for defensive purposes, they could be destroyed by a persistent and strong enemy.

But warfare or the threat of warfare was the exception. In peacetime the ancient city gates were used for multiple purposes.

## II. A Place for Meeting Others and Public Assemblages

Two angels of God met Lot while he "was sitting in the gateway of the city" (Gen 19:1). Boaz deliberately went to the town gate in order to find the next-of-kin to Naomi. Everyone apparently passes through the gate during a day: "Meanwhile Boaz went up to the town gate and sat there. When the kinsman-redeemer he had mentioned came along, Boaz said, "Come over here, my friend, and sit down." So he went over and sat down" (Ruth 4:1). Absalom met people coming to the gate "for justice" and skillfully turned them against his father, David (2 Sam 15:2). While gates were public places, there were dark corners by which a private conversation could go on; but note what Joab did--"Now when Abner returned to Hebron, Joab took him aside into the gateway, as though to speak with him privately. And there, to avenge the blood of his brother Asahel, Joab stabbed him in the stomach, and he died" (2 Sam 3:27). Just beyond many gates were squares where large groups of people could congregate (see Gen 19:2b). In this way Ezra read the Torah to "all the people assembled as one man in the square before the Water Gate" (Neh 8:1). But the ancient city gate complex was for more than just meeting people coming and going, for good or ill.

## III. A Place for Court Proceedings and Legal Transactions

The city gate area was where one went to receive justice, hopefully. Note the instructions in Deuteronomy. The father and mother of a rebellious son "shall take hold of him and bring him to the elders at the gate of his town" to be judged and perhaps even stoned to death (Deut 21:19-21). The parents of their slandered married daughter "shall bring proof that she was a virgin to the town elders at the gate" (Deut 22:15). A widow who seeks levirate marriage by her husband's brother "shall go to the elders at the town gate" in order to receive "justice," either marriage itself or the ability to publicly shame the brother's family (Deut 25:7-10). Sometimes the execution of justice is done in the gate area: "If a man happens to meet in a town a virgin pledged to be married and he sleeps with her, you shall take both of them to the gate of that town and stone them to death" (Deut 22:23-24a).

"Oppression" in the gates was a synonym for judicial corruption. The NIV does not translate *sha'ar* as "gate," but rather "court" in Prov 22:22: "Do not exploit the poor because they are poor and do not crush the needy in court." It literally reads "in the gate." The same kind of interpretive translation is found in Amos 5: "You hate the one who reproves in court [in the gate]" (vs. 10a); "You oppress the righteous and take bribes and you deprive the poor of justice in the courts [in the gates]" (vs. 12b); "Hate evil, love good; maintain justice in the courts [in the gates]" (vs. 15a). The same is found in Isaiah: "those who with a word make a man out to be guilty, who ensnare the defender in court [in the gate] and with false testimony deprive the innocent of justice" (29:21). The truly guilty and foolish man cannot defend himself in the court proceedings as Prov 24:7 states: "Wisdom is too high for a fool; in the assembly at the gate he has nothing to say."

But how are we to visualize these court proceedings? Tel Dan is a good example. Usually the judge had a special seat in the gate area as illustrated by Eli (1 Sam 4:18) and Samuel (1 Sam 9:18). Or kings often held court or public audiences for various reasons. King David, when he had finished mourning for his son Absalom, "got up and took his seat in the gateway. When the men were told, 'The king is sitting in the gateway, they all came before him'" (2 Sam 19:8). Jehoshaphat and Ahab sat in the gate of Samaria (1 Kgs 22:10) [an incident we will mention later]. Apparently Zedekiah, the last king of Judah, was holding court "while [he] was sitting in the Benjamin Gate" (Jer 38:7b). (The reference to the "King's Gate" in 1 Chron 9:18 is referring to the temple gate and not the city gate.)

"Elders" were a necessary part of the judicial system. In fact, a seat "among the elders" in the gate was a high honor in those days (Prov 31:23). Job must have been an elder or even a judge in the gate by his own statement: "When I went to the gate of the city and took my seat in the public square... I took up the case of the stranger" (Job 29:7, 16b). When Jeremiah laments: "The elders are gone from the city gate" (Lam 5:14a), he means there are no longer any court proceedings or legal transactions—the city is destroyed along with its inhabitants in exile.

The Book of Ruth instructs us that "Boaz took

ten of the elders of the town and said, 'Sit here,' and
they did so" (Ruth 4:2). Even the archaeologists at
Tel Dan use this scripture to illustrate the use of
the long stone bench parallel to the "throne-seat"
in the Dan gateway. Boaz and the no-name next-
of-kin would have stood in front of the judge/king
and the ten elders and transacted their "legal business." Thus, did Boaz purchase Naomi's husband's
land as well as perform levirate marriage on behalf
of Naomi and Ruth in order to keep Abimelech's
"seed" alive (Ruth 4:7-10). "Then the elders and
all those at the gate said, 'We are witnesses'" (Ruth
4:11a).

These types of legal transactions and court proceedings had a long and enduring tradition as illustrated by Abraham's experience with the Hittites:
"Ephron the Hittite was sitting among his people
and he replied to Abraham in the hearing of all the
Hittites who had come to the gate of his city. "No,
my lord," he said, "Listen to me; I give you the
field, and I give you the cave that is in it. I give
it to you in the presence of my people. Bury your
dead" (Gen 23:10-11). After the essential cultural
hassling over a gracious gift or a legal payment, the
text reads: "So Ephron's field in Machpelah near
Mamre—both the field and the cave in it, and all the
trees within the borders of the field—was deeded to
Abraham as his property in the presence of all the
Hittites who had come to the gate of the city" (Gen
23:17-18). Incidentally, it cost Abraham 400 shek-
els of silver! Not a very good deal.

## IV. A Place for Prophetic Proclamation

Besides the activities of kings and judges, the prophets often shared their messages in the city gates, for that was where the people were. On one occasion prophets were summoned by the king or kings in this case. "Dressed in their royal robes, the king of Israel [Ahab] and Jehoshaphat king of Judah were sitting on their thrones at the threshing floor by the entrance of the gate of Samaria, with all the prophets prophesying before them" (1 Kgs 22:10). About 400 "false" prophets were there; but only one, the true prophet Micaiah, spoke the truth to the two kings!

Jeremiah is told by Yahweh to go stand "at the gate of the people, through which the kings of Judah go in and out; stand also at all the other gates of Jerusalem," in order to warn them against doing business on the Sabbath; i.e., "Be careful not to carry a load on the Sabbath day or bring it through the gates of Jerusalem" (Jer 17:19, 21).

"Wisdom" is personified in Proverbs as calling out to the young man to hold on to the knowledge and fear of Yahweh, presumably as the prophet would cry out: "Wisdom calls aloud in the street, she raises her voice in the public squares; at the head of the noisy streets she cries out, in the gateways of the city she makes her speech" (Prov 1:20-21).

Interestingly, as a side-note, the city gate was also a place for "mad-men" and the town's "good-for-nothings." The future king David, himself,

faked madness at the city gate of Gath (1 Sam
21:13). The Psalmist cries that he is the object of
scorn by drunkards' songs at the gate: "Those who
sit at the gate mock me, and I am the song of the
drunkards" (Ps 69:12).

## V. The Marketplace

Finally, closely connected to the city gate was the
marketplace, just outside the gate. Especially during peace time the whole city gate complex made
an excellent marketplace as people went in and
out of the gates during the day. One biblical reference refers to this phenomenon: 2 Kgs 7:1ff. Ben-
Hadad, king of Aram, besieged Samaria and there
was a great famine in Samaria with food prices
"sky high." Elisha, however, predicted: "About this
time tomorrow, a seah of flour will sell for a shekel
and two seahs of barley for a shekel at the gate of
Samaria," which was the marketplace! [See 2 Kgs
7 for this interesting story.] We have already mentioned how Jeremiah attempted to stop business
men from carrying their wares on the Sabbath (Jer
17). Nehemiah attempted to do the same. Nehemiah
warned: "Once or twice the merchants and sellers
of all kinds of goods spent the night outside Jerusalem. But I warned them and said, 'Why do you
spend the night by the wall? If you do this again, I
will lay hands on you.' From that time on they no
longer came on the Sabbath" (Neh 13:20-21).

A modern-day example can be found at the
Damascus Gate in Jerusalem. Every day the mul-

titudes of people, mostly tourists, crowd this area and are constantly treated to the selling of foods and other goods just outside the gate, much as it was in ancient times.

## VI. Conclusion: Metaphorical Use of "Gate"

Because of the cultural/historical use of the ancient city gates, the term itself is used metaphorically throughout the biblical literature. The whole process of the administration of justice is termed "at/in the gate" (Prov 22:22; Amos 5:15; Jer 15:7). It is used in metonymy where "gate" stands for the whole city (Gen 22:17; 24:60). Note how this metaphorical use is at the same time personified by Isaiah in a parallel phrase: "Wait, O gate! Howl, O city!" (Isa 14:31a; cp. 3:26).

"Gate" is the symbol of access or entrance to anything such as: "gate of death" (Ps 9:13); "gate of Yahweh" (Ps 118:20); "gate of heaven" (Gen 28:17); or the entrance to a particular land (Jer 15:7; Nah 3:13). Perhaps metonymy is used in Isa 60:11 where the gates "will always stand open," which is in an eschatological sense the gospel. This use can be said of the "gates of righteousness" (Ps 118:19) and the "open gates" for the righteous nation to enter (Isa 26:2). "Gates" are personified in several references: Isa 3:26; 14:31; Jer 14:2; and Ps 24:7, 9. "Gates" are used symbolically throughout Ezek 40-48 and Rev 21 to refer to the Idealized and Perfect City and Temple (the New Jerusalem and the Idealized Temple). **Those who have "citizen's**

rights" and political authority or voice are called
"those who enter the gate" (Gen 23:10; Job 29:7);
the body of citizens within a city can be called "all
the gate of my people" (Ruth 3:11); and men who
are capable of bearing arms, i.e., soldiers, are called
"those who go out the gate" (Gen 34:24).

In light of this study two New Testament concepts can be illuminated. One is Jesus' statement to
Peter: "And I tell you that you are 'Rock,' and on
this rock I will build my church, and the gates of
Hades [Hell] will not overcome it" (Matt 16:18).
This is referring to the "powers" of hell/death/Satan
that cannot overcome the "onslaught" of Christ and
the church. In other words, "the powers of evil cannot contain or hold in check the new community."
[AB, Matthew, Albright, p. 196.] (For concepts of
the "gates of Hades/hell/death" see such passages
as Isa 38:10; Job 17:16; 38:17; Ps 9:13; 107:18; and
in the Apocrypha, Wisdom of Sol 16:13.) The pic-
ture here is the offensive action of the Church and
the defensive posture of the "gates of Hell." As the
church preaches the gospel concerning the resurrection and reign of Jesus, the "power" of Satan "who
holds the power of death" (Heb 2:14) cannot with-
stand the attack. The Church will always overcome
the "gates of hell!" The Church is on the offense
and "Hell" is on the defense! Victory is promised:
John 16:33; Rom 16:20; Eph 6:10-13; Rev 12:13-
16; 17:14; 20:7-10.

For the second insight I quote from Ray Vander
Laan:

The Bible predicts that the Messiah will enter

the temple through this gate [the Eastern/Beautiful Gate]. Years ago, Islamic leaders blocked the entrance and built a cemetery in front of it to prevent the Messiah from entering. If the closed gate would not stop Him, the cemetery would, because as a Jew, the Messiah would become ceremonially unclean if He touched anything connected with death; thus, he would not be able to enter the Temple Mount.

By tradition, the Last Judgment is to take place at this gate. Since city gates were used as courthouses, it is easy to see why the Bible would describe that event in a location like this one. "Believers" would be blessed with entrance into the New Jerusalem. [That The World May Know, Teacher's Guide I, p. 14].

I believe this is symbolically used for the Last Judgment. See such passages as Joel 3:2, 12; Zech 14:1-11; Isa 62:10; and Rev 21.

Now when you read in your Bible text and you come to a "gate," hopefully it will have much more meaning than before. May "your gates" always stand open!"

———————

I believe after reading this very well written review of the usage of ancient city gates, you have gained a deeper understanding of their importance in the lives of the people who depended upon them for their safety as well as the significance they held in their lives by being an access point where many functions necessary to the societal existence played out at these gated areas.

As you now understand, these gated access points were used for much more than entering and exiting. Commerce took place there, as well as refuge. Their court systems functioned in these areas. Kings and prophets spoke at times to the gathering of people within these gated areas. If a person was looking to meet someone, they had a good chance of finding them there, because all who entered or exited the city had to do so through these gates. The city walls and gates could be thick and strongly built, but they weren't fool-proof against the enemy's attack if they weren't maintained properly.

For the Old Covenant Hebrews, this meant not only the maintenance of the physical walls and gates, but being faithful to the Covenant of which they were in agreement with God. Remember it was God who stated under their conditional Covenant that if certain stipulations were met, he would cause it so no man would desire their land, thus giving safety to their borders (see Ex. 34:23-24).

With time, they fell prey to many things that drew them away from their faithfulness to God and the agreement they had made, and this ultimately led to their going into captivity under the rule of foreign nations who had invaded their borders and overthrown their cities. This was how the Hebrews under the Old Covenant fared. God, in His faithfulness kept a remnant, and as promised, brought them back into the land. And even today, the nation of Israel is gathering its people from many nations of the world. God is good and he is faithful.

## *Take Hold of His Strength*

How does all this talk of gates apply to us who are on this side of the cross; which took place nearly two thousand years ago? We don't live in walled cities with gates, (or at least most of us don't) and our enemies aren't trying to gain access through our gates and walls, or are they?

The Old Covenant people were not born again. The nation of Israel was at that time [and remains] a physical kingdom with physical borders and with towns and cities.

We are born-again children of God and the kingdom of God is within us (see Luke 17:21). Hearing the truth of the gospel is how we gained invitation and access into this kingdom. We received the Holy Spirit by the hearing of faith (see Gal. 3:2b). The book of Romans says it this way, "Consequently faith comes from hearing the message, and the message is heard through the word of Christ." (Rom. 10:17 NIV) Some Bible translations say the message is heard through the Word of "God." Now we know that Jesus is God, but if you use the word "God" in this passage of Scripture, that would encompass the entire Bible, including the Old Testament law with its curses. And we know the law is not of faith, but the message of the gospel, the hearing of Christ, brings faith (see Gal. 3:12).

Further, it's stated in the book of Hebrews, "For we

also have had the gospel preached to us, just as they did; but the message they heard was of no value to them, because those who heard did not combine it with faith." (Heb. 4:2 NIV) The gospel is truly "good news" and it's the message that reveals "the Strength we are to take hold of."

So once again, the Scripture in Isaiah bears repeating, "In that day the LORD Almighty will be a glorious crown, a beautiful wreath for the remnant of his people. He will be a spirit of justice to the one who sits in judgment, a source of strength to those who turn back the battle at the gate." (Isa. 28:5-6 NIV) Also, as found earlier in Isaiah: "Or let him take hold of my strength, that he may make peace with me; and he shall make peace with me." (Isa. 27:5 KJV)

If you're born again, you have "made peace with God." (See Rom. 5:1) You've found His strength, you've gained access into the kingdom and the kingdom is inside of you! Now you must defend it. You know the Truth that has set you free (see John 8:32). God says through the Apostle Paul in the book of Galatians, "It is for freedom that Christ has set us free, stand firm, then, and do not let yourselves be burdened again by a yoke of slavery." (Gal. 5:1 NIV)

So, how do we defend or guard against the enemy's attacks? Paul says in the book of Romans,

> "The word is near you; it is in your mouth and in your heart," that is, the word of faith we are proclaiming: That if you confess with your mouth, "Jesus is Lord," and

believe in your heart that God raised him from the dead, you will be saved. For it is with your heart that you believe and are justified, and it is with your mouth that you confess and are saved. (Rom. 10:8b-10 NIV)

This is awesome!

God says, through the Apostle Paul, that the gospel puts the Word in our mouth and in our heart. God is the Word (see John 1:1). And now, as believers, God resides in our hearts. Now the word "heart' here does not refer to our physical heart, but our spirit. He resides in our born-again spirit. Our soul is made up of our mind, will and emotions. So we must recognize that at the new birth or when we were born again, we received a brand new spirit, which is now holy, but our soul, which again is made up of our mind, will and emotions has not yet been renewed. That's why God tells us to do just that in chapter 12 of the book of Romans, where He says, "Do not conform any longer to the pattern of this world, but be transformed by the renewing of your mind." (Rom. 12:2a NIV)

### *Guard Your Heart*

So, in effect, God is saying renew your mind so you understand who and what you are as a child of God, as a born-again Christian. Renew your thinking, so your thought life agrees with the truth of who you [now] are. Why do we need to do this? Well, because we get attacked or assaulted in many ways with lies that try to come against the truth that we are now born-again, spirit-filled, blood-washed saints, who are totally pleasing to God, and who are no longer under the law or conditional Covenant God had with the Old Testament Hebrews, but we are now under the unconditional Covenant of grace, known as the New Covenant or New Testament, put into effect by Christ's shed blood. We are pleasing to Father God because he sees us the same as he sees his Son Jesus (see 1 John 4:17b).

We are now sons and daughters of the Most High God and our names are written in the Lamb's book of life! "But I messed up today." No, you didn't. Remember, can a dead man sin? (See Rom. 6:3) "But, I'm struggling with smoking." Well, if you're born again, you are a righteous smoker. Now... know you're righteous and don't allow yourself to come under the guilt and condemnation of the law, and you'll be walking in the Spirit, (walking in truth) which gives you the power to be released from addictive habits that can harm you.

Remember, the war in our minds or the battle we constantly face, spoken of in Galatians is this: "For the flesh lusteth against the Spirit, and the Spirit against the flesh: and they are contrary the one to the other:" (Gal. 5:17a) And once again, this doesn't mean the flesh wants us to steal, kill, slander, gossip, lie, etc. and the Spirit wants us to go to church, help people, give money to the needy, read our Bibles, etc. It means the flesh wants us to try and gain a righteousness by our own effort; [it thinks it can do it by itself], but the Spirit says the only way you'll ever be righteous or gain the righteousness of God is by putting your faith in Christ, by becoming born again and receiving an imputed righteousness.

"For he hath made him to be sin for us, who knew no sin; that we might be made the righteousness of God in him." (2 Corinthians 5:21)

My hope in writing this chapter titled 'The Gates" is that you would see and realize that if a standard was raised and the Old Testament Hebrews honored God with the proper sacrifices, remaining faithful to the Covenant they had agreed to, a righteous standard would have been met allowing for the protection of their borders as well as their fortified cities. But if this standard was not met, they were unprotected, ultimately leading to the takeover, and in some cases, destruction of their walled cities. For this destruction and ruin to have come upon the people, it had to have first begun as a moral decay from within, a turning away from God's standard, and along with it went the societal moorings that strengthened and protected all levels of society, both family and judicial. For after all "righteousness exalts a nation." We as believers are the temple of God, and the kingdom of God resides in us.

As born-again believers we have received the righteousness of God as a "free gift" and we remain righteous apart from the works of the law. We are in rightstanding with God and at peace with God and we have received the benefits of the cross…freely given, but if we are unaware of this, and let the *enemy come through our gates in the form of lying thoughts*, with the intent of ruining us from within, we will feel like defeated Christians and perhaps fall prey to destructive forces, but we don't have to.

We must man the gates and refute any lying thoughts that come against our righteousness.

I end this chapter with this passage of Scripture from Luke's gospel:

> As he approached Jerusalem and saw the city, he wept over it, and said, "If you, even you, had only known on this day what would bring you peace - but now it is hidden from your eyes, The days will come upon you when your enemies will build an embankment against you and encircle you and hem you in on every side, They will dash you to the ground, you and the children within your walls. They will not leave one stone on another, because you did not recognize the time of God's coming to you. (Luke 19:41-44 NIV)

# THREE

## Imaginations

The word of the Lord came to Jeremiah. God said, "Go and proclaim this in the hearing of Jerusalem" (see Jer. 2:1-2a). God used the prophet Jeremiah to proclaim a lengthy message to the people of Jerusalem. The words of this message are found in the book of Jeremiah, chapters 2:1 through 3:5. Although many things are spoken in this lengthy message, the final two verses really jumped out at me one day as I was reading it.

God, within these verses, is using Jeremiah to voice a question that God is saying the people of Jerusalem are asking of God. Actually, it's a number of questions and it goes like this: "Wilt thou not from this time cry unto me, my Father, thou art the guide of my youth? Will he reserve his anger forever? Will he keep it to the end? Behold thou has spoken and done evil things as thou couldest." Jer. 3:4-5 The New International Version says it this way: "Have you not just called to me: My Father, my friend from my youth, Will you always be angry? Will your wrath continue forever? This is

83

how you talk, but you do all the evil you can."

These questions are very interesting because if you've been in the church for any length of time, you quickly understand a lot of people are seeking guidance or direction for their lives and also struggle with feeling that God is angry with them or wrathful. But here, God is saying these are the questions the people of Jerusalem are about to ask of him. This takes place at a time in Israel's history of approximately 626 to 586 BC. The book of Jeremiah is essentially a collection of prophecies by Jeremiah, addressed primarily to Judah, but also to nine foreign nations.

These prophecies focus mainly on judgment, though there are some concerning restoration. Jeremiah's prophetic ministry was directed to the kingdom of Judah during the last 40 years of its history before going into Babylonian exile. Jeremiah is sometimes referred to as "the weeping prophet" because of his heart for his backsliding countrymen, for although the kingdom of Judah, for the most part, did not heed his prophetic warnings and did go into captivity, the book of Jeremiah also contains [as one of his prophecies] the revelation of the New Covenant; which as we shall see, reveals God's heart for not only the people of Judah, but for all people, and is in one way or another, echoed throughout every book of the Bible (see Jer. 1:1-3 for more information on Jeremiah).

### God's Character in Question

Once again, the questions asked in Jeremiah read as

follows: "Have you not just called to me, 'My Father, my friend from my youth, Will you always be angry? Will your wrath continue forever? This is how you talk, but you do all the evil you can." (Jer. 3:4-5 NIV) God, of course, knows all things, and with these questions the hearts of the people Jeremiah was addressing were revealed. They were about to go into exile and this would be a judgment for unfaithfulness on their part for not living up to the standard of the Old Covenant in which they were under. Yet, the very questions they were about to ask when this happened would expose their thinking, or mindset, that led them there.

Their questions are directed toward God and reference his character, or really, their understanding of his character. As to guidance, they are in essence saying, "God, you used to guide us as a people, where are you now?" And as to anger or wrath, their questions showed that they thought God was a wrathful God, whose wrath and anger might never cease. It was God Himself who gave us the refrain of these people's hearts in the form of these questions, but here in the book of Jeremiah, he not only gives us their questions, but he gives us the answers as well. But before we look at the way he answered the people, let's look at the people themselves.

There are many differences between these people who were under the Old Covenant and we who now enjoy the New Covenant promises. Those people, of course, were before the "work of the cross," so that means the Holy Spirit had not yet been sent. They were spiritually dead. They were not born-again people as are we who now know Christ. The Spirit would come on certain people, such as prophets and kings, at times, before the work of the cross, but they were not born again. As mentioned above, they were in a Covenant relationship with God. As Old Testament saints, they of course were under the Old Covenant, the Covenant of law. And as New Testament saints, (Christians) we are under the Covenant of grace.

The Old Covenant was put into effect with blood, but it was the blood of animals (see Heb. 9:18). The New Testament was made effective by the blood of Christ (see Heb. 9:12). The blood of Christ cleanses the consciences of New Testament believers because Christ died once and rose again, so we are confident that our sin problem has been dealt with, we are guilt-free, with no fear of wrath or punishment (see Heb. 9:26). The Old Testament saints had to repeatedly offer animal sacrifices each time they sinned, and yearly as a nation. This kept the Old Testament saints sin-conscious and keeping short lists of their behavior. If they sinned and didn't offer the prescribed sacrifice, there was the penalty of wrath, under the law.

The book of Hebrews, as well as the book of Leviticus, tells us that without the shedding of blood, there is no forgiveness of sins (see Heb. 9:22b, Lev. 17:11). Both Covenants had priests. The Old Covenant had priests who would eventually die and have to be replaced, or they would be found with a blemish of some sort and have to be removed.

The New Covenant has Jesus as our perfect High Priest, Who will never die again and was found to be without spot or blemish, and always remains faithful. (see Heb. 7:25). The Old Covenant saints were under the law and Scripture says that by the law is the knowledge of sin (see Rom. 3:20). New Testament saints are under **grace** and therefore we have boldness to enter into the holiest by the blood of Jesus, in full assurance of faith (see Heb. 10:19-22). The Old Covenant dealt with types and shadows and the New Covenant deals with New Testament realities.

### *God's Answer*

With this said, let's look at how God answered the peoples refrain. We find it in several locations in the latter chapters of Jeremiah. The first is found in chapter 23, and it reads like this, "The anger of the LORD will not turn back until he fully accomplishes the *purposes of his heart*. In days to come, you will understand it clearly." (Jer. 23:20 NIV) One translation says, we shall consider it perfectly. This passage is found in the King James Version and reads as follows, "The anger of the LORD shall not return, until he have executed, and 'til he have performed the thoughts of his heart: in the latter days ye shall consider it perfectly." (Jer. 23:20)

Then again, found further back in the book of Jeremiah, he similarly states, "The fierce anger and indignation of the LORD shall not turn back until he has executed and accomplished the *thoughts and intents of*

*his mind and heart.* In the latter days ye shall understand this." (Jer. 30:24 AMP) How cool is this? This
of course is referencing the New Covenant that we as
born-again saints are living under today. We are living
in the latter days.

The New Covenant's future arrival is revealed pro-
phetically by the prophet Jeremiah in chapter 31,
which is a Covenant God swore by oath. Hebrews
7:22 (NIV) states, "Because of this oath, Jesus has become the guarantee of a better covenant." The New
Covenant, which is proclaimed in the book of Jeremiah as a future event, is stated as present day reality in
the epistle to the Hebrews and once again reads, "This
is the Covenant I will make with them after that time,
says the LORD. I will put my laws in their hearts,
and I will write them on their minds." Then he adds:
"Their sins and lawless acts I will remember no more."
And where these have been forgiven, there is no longer any sacrifice for sin." (Heb. 10:16-18 NIV) God is
just in making this New Covenant, because *the wrath
that was against mankind's sin was placed on Jesus as our
sacrifice.*

Jesus said in John's gospel, "And I, if I be lifted up
from the earth, will draw all *men* unto me. This he said
signifying what death he should die." (John 12:32-
33) But, it's interesting to note though, that the word
"men" in verse 32 is italicized. This indicates it was
added by the Bible translators. It should say, "and I, if
I be lifted up from the earth, will draw 'all' unto me."
This entire passage, John 12:31-34, is in the context of

judgment. Jesus is saying that when he is placed on the cross, all the judgment for man's sin will be placed on him. The entire wrath of God toward mankind's sin will be [was] put on Him on the cross.

He would act as a lightning rod, and that is exactly what happened. The wrath of God has been satisfied by the shed blood of Jesus; by His atonement made for the sins of the world (see 1 John 2:2). This is why we, as New Covenant believers, should no longer have fear or torment, because we have been perfected by love!

As stated in John's epistle, "There is no fear in love. But perfect love drives out fear, because fear has to do with punishment. The one who fears is not made perfect in love." (1 John 4:18 NIV) There is no longer punishment as the Old Covenant saints experienced. That's the "good news". We have peace with God. And as ambassadors, God has given us the ministry of reconciliation, "That is, that God was in Christ reconciling the world to Himself, not imputing their trespasses to them, and has committed to us the word of reconciliation." "For he made him who knew no sin to be sin for us, that we might become the righteousness of God in him." (2 Cor. 5:19, 21 NKJV)

God said in the book of Psalms,

> Today if you hear his voice, do not harden your hearts as you did at Meribah, as you did that day at Massah in the desert, where your fathers tested and tried me, though they had seen what I did. For 40 years I was angry with that generation; I said, "They

> are a people whose hearts go astray, and
> they have not known my ways. (Ps. 95:8-
> 10 NIV)

Scripture tells us that only two from that generation came into the Promised Land with the younger
generation. Now remember as discussed earlier, these
people chose to put themselves under the Old Covenant of law. They chose to enter into agreement with
God, saying in their pride that they could keep all of
the law (see Ex.19:7-8). And their words and acts,
which maligned God's character, further revealed their
hearts, saying things such as found in Deuteronomy,
"And ye murmured in your tents, and said, 'Because
the Lord hated us, he hath brought us forth out of
the land of Egypt, to deliver us into the hand of the
Amorites, to destroy us.'" (Deut. 1:27) Also, as found
in Exodus, "And he received them at their hand, and
fashioned it with a graving tool, after he had made it
a molten calf: and they said, These be thy gods, oh Israel, which brought thee up out of the land of Egypt."
(Ex. 32:4)

### *Imaginary vs. Reality*

These types of words and acts depicted the hearts of
many of the people of Israel; fortunately not all of
them, for there was a faithful remnant. But it's obvi-
ous that many didn't know God or understand him,
and this mindset plagued the Israelites long after they
entered the Promised Land. Sadly, they often acted as
if they had no hope.

God said to Jeremiah,

> Now therefore go to, speak to the men of
> Judah, and to the inhabitants of Jerusalem,
> saying, thus saith the Lord; Behold, I frame
> evil against you, and devise a device against
> you: return ye now every one from his evil
> way, and make your ways and your doings
> good. And they said, There is no hope: but
> we will walk after our own devices, and we
> will every one do the imagination of his
> evil heart. (Jer. 18:11-12)

If you are trusting in your own performance, there
**is no** hope. This was the refrain of many in Israel at
that time whom eventually were killed or carried off
into exile. Scripture says it is the goodness of God that
leads us to repentance (see Rom. 2:4). Remember,
"repentance" simply means to change how you think.
Most of these people really didn't know or understand
God, although they witnessed many of the miracles
God used in delivering them from the bondage and
slavery of Egypt (see Ps. 103:7). The problem was that
although God took the Jewish people out of slavery, it
didn't take the slavery out of the Jewish people. Many
of them were so accustomed to a dire existence that
they couldn't recognize real freedom and how to es-
cape emotionally from their former captivity.

Zoo animals that have spent most of their lives in
cages, pacing back and forth, when released into the
larger open areas of a more modern zoo have been
known to limit themselves to a small area the size of

their former cage, pacing back and forth in the same restricted space, but it's an imaginary space. It's not reality. They could be free to roam about, but the years of confinement have shaped their mentality and therefore their behavior. So it was for most who came out of Egypt.

Remember, when we were born naturally, we were born "spiritually dead" and we didn't know the things of God (see 1 Cor. 2:14). We didn't know the kindness of God. Some of us had some pretty good families with pretty good parents and siblings, but some of us did not. It can be a pretty cruel world out there with peer pressure and dysfunctional families and we all learn how to survive. Apart from God, it's a dog-eat-dog world and that's what we all were – we were apart from God. But now we have been brought near by the blood of Christ (see Col. 1:20, Eph. 2:13).

When the Pharisees asked Jesus when the kingdom of God would come, Jesus said, "Neither shall they say, Lo here! Or, lo there! For, behold, the kingdom of God is within you." (Luke 17:21)  If you are born again, you are the temple of God. If you are born again, you are pleasing to God, at peace with God. So, just what are God's thoughts toward us?

Well, when God delivered us from darkness and brought us into light, (see Col. 1:12-13) God brought us into the kingdom of His dear son. When God said, through the prophet Jeremiah, "The anger of the Lord will not turn back until he fully accomplishes the purposes of his heart," (Jer. 23:20a NIV) or as in chapter

30 of Jeremiah, "The fierce anger and indignation of the Lord shall not turn back until he has executed and accomplished the thoughts and intents of his mind and heart," (Jer. 30:24a AMP) what did he mean? As stated earlier, this is referring to the "work of the cross."

It bears repeating what the Apostle Paul said in the book of Romans,

> For when we were yet without strength, in due time Christ died for the ungodly. For scarcely for a righteous man will one die: yet peradventure for a good man some would even dare to die. But God commendeth his love toward us, in that, while we were yet sinners, Christ died for us. Much more then, being now justified by his blood, we shall be saved from wrath through him. For if, when we were enemies, we were reconciled to God by the death of his Son, much more, being reconciled, we shall be saved by his life. And not only so, but we also joy in God through our Lord Jesus Christ, by whom we have now received the atonement." (Rom. 5:6-11)

Praise God!

### God's Thoughts Toward You

Is your joy in God? It can be if you understand that you have been saved from God's wrath and you are now under grace, and you enter into this grace through faith in Christ. When you do this, you are translated from darkness to light; you are made new and found totally pleasing to God. When Father God looks at us, he sees his Son, because we are covered in his Son's blood.

It says in John's first epistle, "Herein is our love made perfect, that we may have boldness in the Day of Judgment: because as he is, so are we in this world." (1 John 4:17 ) The way that God thinks of his Son Jesus is the same way he thinks of you. This blessing is a free gift, but you must become born again to receive it. His love is extended toward all. He is not mad or angry at you. If you are struggling with something, a behavior you know isn't right, God says come as you are. Know that God is a *kind and merciful God* who has already forgiven mankind, but you and I must receive it (see Ps. 86:5).

What are God's thoughts and the intents of his heart toward us? Let's examine some Scriptures found in the Word of God. One popular verse used in many graduation cards, and I believe the King James Version of this verse best expresses God's heart, reads as follows: "For I know the thoughts that I think towards you, saith the Lord, *thoughts of peace, and not of evil, to give you an expected end.*" (Jer. 29:11) Another translation says it this way: "For I know the plans I have for you," declares the Lord, "plans to prosper you and not to harm you, plans to give you hope and a future." (NIV) I believe God does have good plans for us, but I believe when we know and understand that God is a good God, who is thinking favorable thoughts towards us, those plans are more apt to be fulfilled.

As found in the book of Isaiah,

> And all thy children shall be taught of the Lord; and great shall be the peace of thy children. In righteousness shalt thou be established: thou shalt be far from oppression; for thou shalt not fear: and from terror; for it shall not come near thee. Behold, they shall surely gather together, but not by me: whosoever shall gather together against thee shall fall for thy sake. Behold, I have created the smith that bloweth the coals in the fire, and that bringeth forth an instrument for his work; and I have created the waster to destroy. No weapon that is formed against thee shall prosper; and every tongue that shall rise against thee in judgment **thou shalt condemn**. This is the heritage of the servants of the LORD, and their righteousness is of me, saith the LORD. (Isa. 54:13-17, emphasis mine)

Understand that some bad things do happen on this planet, for Jesus Himself said, "These things I have spoken unto you, that in Me ye might have peace. In the world ye shall have tribulation: but be of good cheer; I have overcome the world." (John 16:33) He also says earlier in the gospel of John, "The thief cometh not, but for to steal, and to kill, and to destroy: I am come that they might have life, and that they might have it more abundantly." (John 10:10) *We must stop attributing the works of the devil to God and understand that God is a good God who loves us and thinks kindly towards us and does not want to harm us, but only wants the best for us* and has done everything necessary to provide what we need. As stated in the book of Psalms, "Many, OH LORD my God, are thy wonderful works which thou hast done, and thy thoughts which are to usward: they cannot be reckoned up in order unto thee: if I would declare and speak of them, they are more than can be numbered." (Ps. 40:5)

Further we find, "But I am poor and needy; yet the Lord thinketh upon me: thou art my help and my deliverer; make no tarrying, Oh my God." (Ps. 40:17), and elsewhere in Psalms, "The counsel of the Lord standeth forever, the thoughts of his heart through all generations." (Ps. 33:11) God spoke through the prophet Jeremiah in chapter 24,

> For *I will set mine eyes upon them for good,* and I will bring them again to this land: and I will build them, and not pull them down; and I will plant them, and not pluck them up. And **I will give them an heart to know Me**, that I am the LORD: and they shall be my people, and I will be their God: for they shall return unto me with their whole heart. (Jer. 24:6-7, emphasis mine )

### *Our Hearts Have Been Sprinkled*

The "heart to know me" that God speaks of here is the

new heart of flesh we have received when we became born again (see Ez. 11:19). Our heart is no longer deceitfully wicked (see Jer. 17:9). For as God speaks through the prophet Jeremiah concerning what will eventually happen because of the work of the cross, He says, "At that time they shall call Jerusalem the throne of the LORD; and all the nations shall be gathered unto it, to the name of the LORD, to Jerusalem: neither shall they walk any more after the imagination of their evil heart." (Jer. 3:17)

The Old Covenant saints were under the covenant of law and it states in Hebrews,

> For the law having a shadow of good things to come, and not the very image of the things, can never with those sacrifices which they offered year by year continually make the comers thereunto perfect. For then would they not have ceased to be offered? Because that *the worshippers once purged should have no more conscience of sins.*" (Heb. 10:1-2, italics mine)

Further in Hebrews we read, "And having an high priest over the house of God; Let us draw near with a true heart in full assurance of faith, *having our hearts sprinkled from an evil conscience,* and our bodies washed with pure water." (Heb. 10:21-22, italics mine) Therefore, now we can do what it says in Proverbs, and that is to "Trust in the LORD with all thine heart; and lean not unto thine own understanding, in all thy ways acknowledge him, and he shall direct thy paths." (Prov.

3:5-6) This is the guidance that the Hebrew children sought after.

The word "imagination" is mentioned approximately eight times in the book of Jeremiah. But the first time it's mentioned is in the book of Genesis, "And God saw that the wickedness of man was great in the earth, and that every imagination of the thoughts of his heart was only evil continually." (Gen. 6:5) This behavior preceded the flood that God brought on the earth. God promised He would never flood the earth again and the wrath for mankind's sin has been placed on Jesus, so in this "dispensation of grace" God is not judging the world or imputing wrath to the world. There is a time coming at the end of the age, where the wrath of God will come on the world, but at that time *the world won't be judged because of sin*, for sin has already been judged. It will be judged for **unbelief**, to those who fail to put their trust in Christ (see John 16:8-11).

For those of us who are believers, we can agree with the Word of God, as stated in the book of Romans, "But God be thanked, that ye were the servants of sin, but ye have obeyed from the heart that form of doctrine which was delivered you." (Rom. 6:17) We as born-again Christians now have a clean heart and a clear conscience, and it's our duty to control our thought life to guard against anything that speaks contrary to this truth. Once again, as discussed in the previous chapter, the war that takes place in our minds is the flesh lusting against the Spirit and the Spirit lusting against the flesh. What this means is the flesh is saying it can be righteous by itself, which is false. And the Spirit is saying the only righteousness we can ever have is through faith in Christ, which of course is true.

The Apostle Paul states in the book of Romans, "Since they show that the requirements of the law are written on their hearts, their consciences also bearing witness, and their thoughts now accusing, now even defending them. This will take place on the day when God will judge men's secrets through Jesus Christ, as my gospel declares." (Rom. 2:15-16 NIV) Let us be found faithful in not allowing our thoughts or hearts to accuse us, but rather to *assure us.*

# FOUR

## Repentance – No Gamble

Due to the significance of and the confusion in the church surrounding the word "repentance," I chose to include this chapter to help clarify some of the misunderstandings surrounding this topic.

I believe Jesus Himself offered one of the best definitions of the word "repentance" when He stated in Matthew 12:41 that the men of Nineveh repented at the preaching of Jonah. I grew up in a denomination that loosely taught that the prophet Jonah went in and told the people of Nineveh to repent. In this famous Bible story, a big fish swallows Jonah and later deposits him alive on the shore. Perhaps, as a young person, you heard the story explained this way, too. When Jesus said the men of Nineveh repented at the preaching of Jonah, we must ask ourselves, what exactly did the prophet Jonah preach to them and how did the people of Nineveh respond?

This story is revealed in the book of Jonah, found in the Old Testament. It's a short book, only four chapters in length, yet it has much to say concerning many topics. The book of Jonah describes the city of Nineveh as having more than 120,000 people who could not tell their right hand from their left (see Jonah 4:11). God had told the prophet Jonah to "go to the great city of Nineveh and preach against it, because its wickedness has come up before me." (Jonah 1:2 NIV) The reluctancy of the prophet Jonah to heed God's request to go to the people of Nineveh is a fascinating study, but I wish to focus on what took place when he (Jonah) finally did obey God's request and how the people of Nineveh responded.

The Bible tells us, "Then the Word of the LORD came to Jonah a second time, 'Go to the great city of Nineveh and proclaim to it the message I give you.'" (Jonah 3:1-2 NIV) The city of Nineveh was of such a size that it required three days for the prophet Jonah to traverse it. As he did, the message of God Jonah proclaimed to the people of Nineveh was simply this, "Forty more days and Nineveh will be overturned." (Jonah 3:4b NIV) When Jesus said that the men of Nineveh repented at the preaching of Jonah, this is what the people heard; "Forty more days and Nineveh will be overturned." We are then told in the verse that follows, "The Ninevites believed God." (Jonah 3:5a NIV)

### Trusting God to be Merciful

What this Scripture is saying is that the people of Nineveh believed that what the prophet Jonah was speaking to them were, in fact, God's words. This belief on the part of the king of Nineveh moved the king to decree a time of fasting and a time of calling out to God for all of Nineveh's people. What was spoken by the king of Nineveh in the entirety of this decree reveals his uncertainty of God's character. The king went on to say, "Let them give up their evil ways and their violence. Who knows? God may yet relent and with compassion turn from His fierce anger so that we will not perish." (Jonah 3:8b-9, NIV)

The king, in doing and saying this, took a chance on God's mercy. Perhaps some fled the city. The Word of God does not tell us if this was so, but the king could have chosen to flee if he had wanted to. In the king's uncertainty, he took a gamble on God's character, which ultimately revealed a merciful God. Repenting, for the king and the people of Nineveh, did not mean coming to God and confessing all their evil behavior, but relying on God's merciful character and nature. Relying on God, or looking to the faithfulness of God's character, is putting your hope and trust in God and believing in His inherent goodness (see Heb. 3:12, Rom. 2:4).

The prophet Jonah was an Old Testament prophet, which meant he was under the Old Covenant law; yet God's nature never changes. The difference for us now is that we are under the New Covenant, and the work of the cross has delivered us from the law and the penalty of breaking the law. God's mercy is extended toward all who rely on Him. This is the certainty we have in Christ.

It's interesting to note that even God repented in the story of Jonah (remember, repentance means to change the direction of your thinking.) Scripture tells us, "When God saw what they did and how they turned from their evil ways, He had compassion and did not bring upon them the destruction He had threatened." (Jonah 3:10, NIV) God had relented as the king of Nineveh had hoped. He (God) changed the direction of His thinking, yet the whole time God was without sin.

So it is for us who are born-again. We are the righteousness of God and God is no longer holding our sin against us. We've received an imputed righteousness or right-standing with God that is apart from the works of the law or our own merit and human effort. As born-again saints, we are no longer under the condemnation of the law, and if we fail, we are free from the punishment of the law that the Old Testament Hebrews were under. Our consciences remain clean. This is the *glorious liberty* we have been delivered into.

Hebrews 3:12 says, "Take heed, brethren, lest there be in any of you an *evil heart of unbelief*, in departing from the living God." (italics mine)

Romans 2:4 (NKJV) says, "Or do you despise the riches of His goodness, forbearance, and longsuffering, not knowing that *the goodness of God leads you to repentance?*" (italics mine)

# Conclusion

In summary, the ***strength*** we are to take hold of is found only in Christ. He enables us to do great things. A person could win the lottery, but he might be a person who is bound by addiction and an uncontrolled lifestyle. He now has the money to possibly do greater harm to himself. True riches are found in knowing Christ and the freedom He offers. This freedom brings real and lasting joy and thankfulness which is the only true and abundant life. Just as the apostles [whom when released from the jail that bound them, were told to do by the angel], let us do likewise and "tell the people the full message of this new life." (see Acts 5:20b, NIV)

I conclude this book with Psalm 100 and Gen.22:17b:

> Make a joyful noise unto the LORD, all ye lands, Serve the LORD with gladness: come before his presence with singing. Know ye that the LORD he is God: it is he that hath made us, and not we ourselves; we are his people, and the sheep of his pasture. Enter into his gates with thanksgiving, and into his courts with praise: be thankful unto him, and bless his name. For

the LORD is good; his mercy is everlasting; and his truth endureth to all generations.

"...and your descendants shall possess the gate of their enemies." (NKJV)

Now... man the gates and be blessed!

# Faith Comes by Hearing

2 Corinthians 5:21, New King James Version (NKJV):

> For He made Him who knew no sin to be
> sin for us, that we might become the righ-
> teousness of God in Him.

1 Peter 3:18, New King James Version (NKJV):

> For Christ also suffered once for sins, the
> just for the unjust, that He might bring us
> to God, being put to death in the flesh but
> made alive by the Spirit,

Romans 5:8, New King James Version (NKJV):

> But God demonstrates His own love to-
> ward us, in that while we were still sinners,
> Christ died for us.

Romans 10:9-10, New King James Version (NKJV):

> [9] that if you confess with your mouth the
> Lord Jesus and believe in your heart that
> God has raised Him from the dead, you
> will be saved. [10] For with the heart one
> believes unto righteousness, and with the
> mouth confession is made unto salvation.

2 Corinthians 5:17, New King James Version (NKJV):

> Therefore, if anyone is in Christ, he is a new creation; old things have passed away; behold, all things have become new.

# Salvation Prayer

Jesus, I know that I can't save myself. Apart from You I am spiritually dead, but I come to You today to receive LIFE ~ eternal life. I know that You are the Son of God and You died for my sin.

I know that even though You died, You rose to newness of life to provide life for all mankind – to those who put their trust in You and call upon Your name. Jesus, I give You my life… take my life and do something with it.

Now, go and tell someone that you made Jesus Lord of your life, and begin your new life by reading the New Testament book of John.

# Bibliography/References

Unless otherwise indicated, all Scripture quotations are from the King James Version of the Holy Bible. (KJV)

Outreach Ministries- Authorized King James Version Copyright © 1998 by Gospel Crusade, Inc. (KJV)

King James Version © 1974, 1976 Thomas Nelson, Inc. Nashville, TN (KJV)

Amplified Bible Copyright ©1954, 1958, 1962, 1964, 1965, 1987 by the Lockman Foundation/Biblegateway.com (AMP)

Men's Devotional Bible – The New International Version Copyright © 1993 by the Zondervan Corp. (NIV)

New International Version 1984 (NIV1984) Holy Bible, New International Version® NIV® Copyright © 1972, 1978, 1984 by Biblica, Inc.®

New International Version UK (NIVUK) Holy Bible, New International Version® Anglicized, NIV® Copyright © 1979, 1984, 2011 by Biblica, Inc.®

New King James Version (NKJV) The Holy Bible New King James Version Copyright © 1982 Thomas

Nelson, Inc.

"What About 1 John 1:9?" By Bob George, People to People Ministries © 2002

"Ancient City Gates" by Dr. Walter D Zorn, http://www.lincolnchristian.edu/directory/people/documents/zorn-city-gates.pdf

www.ingramcontent.com/pod-product-compliance
Lightning Source LLC
Chambersburg PA
CBHW062003040426

42447CB00010B/1886